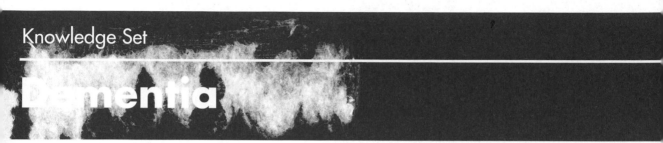

Knowledge Set

Dementia

Caroline Bartle

www.harcourt.co.uk

✓ Free online support
✓ Useful weblinks
✓ 24 hour online ordering

01865 888118

D0294234

Heinemann

From Harcourt

Heinemann, is an imprint of Harcourt Education Limited,
a company incorporated in England and Wales, having its
registered office: Halley Court, Jordan Hill, Oxford, OX2 8EJ.
Registered company number: 3099304
Heinemann is the registered trademark of Harcourt Education Ltd

© Caroline Bartle

First published 2007

12 11 10 09 08 07
10 9 8 7 6 5 4 3 2 1

British Library Cataloguing in Publication Data is available
from the British Library on request.

13-digit ISBN: 978 0 43540230 3

Typeset by TexTech International Private Ltd
Printed by Ashford Colour Press Ltd
Illustrated by Sam Thompson/Calow&Craddock and TexTech
International Private Ltd
Cover design by David Poole
Cover photo: © Lottie Davies/Flowerphotos

Websites
Please note that the examples of websites suggested in this book
were up to date at the time of writing. We have made all links
available on the Heinemann website at www.heinemann.co.uk/
hotlinks. When you access the site, the express code is 2307P.

Contents

Introduction

Knowledge sets have been created by Skills for Care and Development, part of the sector skills council. The idea behind each knowledge set is to provide key learning outcomes for specific areas of work within adult social care. This means that employers and training providers can use a knowledge set to provide in-house training as part of employees' continuing professional development. The advantage of using a knowledge set for the basis of training is that both employers and those who have undertaken training can be assured that a minimum standard has been reached. The knowledge sets also ensure consistency in knowledge and understanding across organisations and services.

The knowledge set for dementia is aimed at those working in social care and handling medication. This book has been written by Caroline Bartle, who started her career in social work and is now Managing Director of New Generation Services, developing services and training for this area. Using this book, in conjunction with the Skills for Care knowledge set, will:

- provide essential learning for all aspects of working with people with dementia, improving confidence and skills
- improve practice in order to meet the individual needs of those who receive care, allowing the opportunity to make a real difference
- support those completing NVQ and other training, providing evidence for portfolios
- support transition between different service settings in the social care sector
- ensure up to date and good practice.

The book is divided into the four main areas of the knowledge set:

- Support individuals with dementia.
- Roles, responsibilities and boundaries.
- Defining dementia.
- Legislation and guidance relevant to individuals with dementia.

These sections are further broken down into manageable topics, with spreads covering one or more learning outcomes. The following features have been designed to enhance the learning experience:

 Activities – completion of the suggested activities and tasks will develop understanding and skills.

 Care scenarios – real-life situations allowing knowledge to be put into practice.

 Look it up – pointers to recognised reference sources that allow comparison of current knowledge with accepted good practice. You may also be asked to investigate your care setting's current procedures and practices.

 Reflection – explore your level of knowledge as well as your thoughts, actions and behaviours.

Remember – key concepts and facts are highlighted and reinforced.

Question check – test your understanding and recall of a topic.

Space has often been provided for note-taking or the completion of activities and tables, although a notebook or workbook can be used alongside this book in order to expand on certain areas.

This book not only covers the learning outcomes for those undertaking training, but also includes a section for those developing or leading training sessions. The Trainer notes provide the answers to Care scenarios, guidance on the completion of activities and also expands on the knowledge given in the four main knowledge set areas. In addition, guidance on activities within the book often include ideas and suggestions for developing an activity and expanding on learning opportunities. Useful icons appear with each activity guidance feature, suggesting how long to spend on the activity and any materials that will be needed (e.g. pens, flip chart, OHP).

The Student log section of this book details all four main areas of the knowledge set for dementia, along with the learning outcomes. Space is provided for trainees to log their progress and record those learning outcomes they have covered. In addition, the tables can also be used to map the content of this book against NVQ courses and any other relevant training being undertaken.

If those completing training are working with younger people with dementia, alcohol-related dementias or learning disabilities, it is recommended that this book is used in conjunction with specific guidance on the issues that affect these groups.

Used either as part of a training package or own its own by an individual, this *Knowledge Set: Dementia* will prove to be an invaluable resource for those developing their career in the adult social care sector.

Acknowledgements

Harcourt would like to thank Skills for Care for giving permission to reproduce the tables of learning outcomes used in the student log section of this book (see pages 113–9).

The publisher and author would like to thank Jenny Chen, Education and Development Manager at The Bath Royal United Hospital, for her constructive review of this book.

The author dedicates this book to: Cathie, Jill and Alan for their contribution to the individual's perspective on the experience of dementia – without you this book would not be whole; to Dr Gill Livingstone and Brenda Bowe for inspiring a passion for dementia care in my early years of practice; to Elaine Woodward for her contributions to loss and change, and her experiences as a carer; to Melanie Frankland (herbalist) for her contribution on alternative therapies within dementia care. The author would also like to thank the publisher, Pen Gresford: thanks for finding me.

Photos

Harcourt would like to thank the following for their kind permission to reproduce images in this book:

J. Chappell/Bubbles – page 37; Neal and Molly Jansen/Alamy – page 87; Photodisc – page 41; Photofusion – pages 5a (Karen Robinson), pp 5b (David Tothill)

1 Support individuals with dementia

1.1 Understand the need for a person-centred and strengths-based approach to the support and well-being of individuals with dementia

In this section you will learn how to build relationships to work with people with dementia in a positive way that is accepting and valuing, and understanding of their needs.

The following was written by someone in the early stages of **Alzheimer's disease.**

Many people when they are talking to someone with Alzheimer's treat them as though they are complete idiots. It is ignorance on their part, which hopefully is what this training manual will help change. On the other hand, just because we can repeat a thing immediately afterwards does not mean we will be able to remember it in a few hours. People who are looking after you obviously think you will remember it and are angry if you don't. Friends and family can be hurtful. It's not being silly, we really, really want to remember.

We want to make our own decisions, and people assume we can't. People sometimes talk over our heads and say 'What does he/she want?' They say we don't look any different – how do they expect us to look? People sometimes just simply don't believe we have Alzheimer's, because we look too normal or too young. They get a shock when they find out. We appreciate help from others, but we don't want to be treated like children. It is just an illness like any other illness – they wouldn't treat us like that if it was anything else.

Source: Cathie, Jill and Alan at the Alzheimer's Forum (a website run by and for people with dementia based at the West Kent branch of the Alzheimer's Society)

Alzheimer's disease

the most common form of dementia; a progressive condition where brain cells die

You can find out more about the Alzheimer's Forum by visiting their website, which you can access by going to www.heinemann. co.uk/hotlinks and entering the express code 2307P.

Activity 1

Read the sentences in the following table. Write in the spaces how they make you feel. Do the words surprise you? Does it make you want to provide better care?

Many people when they are talking to someone with Alzheimer's treat them as though they are complete idiots.	
Just because we can repeat a thing immediately afterwards does not mean we will be able to remember it in a few hours. People who are looking after you obviously think you will remember it and are angry if you don't.	
Friends and family can be hurtful. It's not being silly, we really, really want to remember.	
We want to make our own decisions, and people assume we can't.	
People sometimes talk over our heads and say 'What does he/she want?'	
They say we don't look any different – how do they expect us to look?	
People sometimes just simply don't believe we have Alzheimer's, because we look too normal or too young. They get a shock when they find out.	
It is just an illness like any other illness – they wouldn't treat us like that if it was anything else.	

What you need to learn

- Seeing the person first before seeing the dementia.
- The importance of keeping to a value base of care.
- Helping a person with dementia to make decisions about their care.
- Action to take where a person is unable to make informed choices.
- The importance of developing a person-to-person relationship.
- How loss and change are commonly experienced by people with dementia.
- The importance of having a good understanding of the person's needs.
- How to involve people with dementia in the planning of their care.

Seeing the person first before seeing the dementia

This section helps you to identify common assumptions about people with dementia. It asks you to think about how these ideas affect your behaviour.

Activity 2

In the table below write the words that first come into your head when you think about someone with dementia. In the second column write how, by thinking about a person in this way, you might behave towards them.

Words	Actions

Over time, many false ideas have been created about people who have dementia and this has influenced the way that we see them. Some of these myths include:

- people with dementia are 'mad'
- people with dementia are like babies
- people with dementia always become aggressive
- people with dementia are not able to make any choices.

Think about the impact these perceptions may have on the way that you deliver care.

If you have fixed ideas about people with dementia it will influence the way that you behave towards them. It is important to see the person first and the dementia second.

Activity 3

When you see someone with dementia, do you see the person or the dementia first? Look at the photographs below. Which person do you think has dementia? Why did you make this decision?

What act sets out the rights which people should have?

What values are stated in your organisation's mission statement or charter of rights?

The importance of working to a value base of care

This section helps you to understand what values are important in your role and how you might use them to support the person with dementia.

Value base of care

Enable

to make something able to happen

Proactive

to plan ahead and take action before an event happens, as opposed to responding to the event

As a care worker your role is to **enable** and support a person to live an independent and fulfilled life. This is particularly important when you care for someone with dementia, as they often experience an overwhelming sense of loss of control. As a care worker you must take an enabling and **proactive** approach to help make up for this loss of control. Your role is to help the person achieve a sense of well-being.

In order to provide this kind of care you must first develop the foundations for a positive relationship with the person with dementia. It is important to remember that you must see the person first and the dementia second. Positive relationships are built by valuing the individual's strengths and abilities. The aim of effective care is to promote people's rights (see spider diagram) and build on existing strengths. If care is delivered in this way it can be an enriching experience both for the person with dementia and yourself.

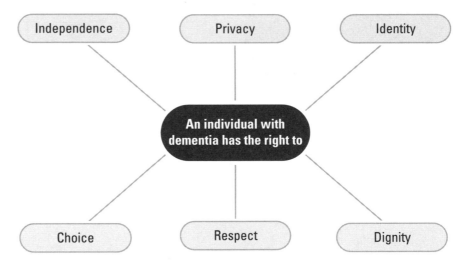

Independence Privacy Identity

An individual with dementia has the right to

Choice Respect Dignity

The rights a person in your care has

Dignity

The dignity of a person with dementia can be affected in a physical way, for example by not providing adequate privacy during personal care, or in an emotional way, for example making fun of people. Memory failure may mean the individual says something that is not factually correct. Care workers should not challenge them as it can leave the person with dementia feeling confused, lost and anxious.

You can do the following to promote a person's dignity:

- value what the person says even if you have a different point of view
- ensure that all personal care is delivered in a dignified way.

Activity 4

Give an example of how you can demonstrate each of the following rights in the table below.

Right	Example
Dignity	By ensuring that privacy is provided when carrying out personal care tasks
Identity	
Respect	
Choice	
Independence	
Privacy	

Identity

A person with dementia faces ongoing changes in and losses of identity. In the later stages of the illness the individual may not even recognise their own face in a mirror. This is made worse by living in a communal residential setting, where there may be no or little reminder of the person's previous life and the experiences that they have had.

You can do the following things to support the identity of a person with dementia:

- call the person by their preferred name
- get to know about their life – learn about what is important to them
- talk with them about their life (this also builds on their strengths)
- make sure that the care that you provide takes account of their culture
- ensure that their environment is arranged in a way that reaffirms their identity – for example photos of their family
- make sure that they have a choice about what clothes they wear.

Respect

Respect is not automatic but needs to be demonstrated through a **person-centred** approach to care in every encounter with the person with dementia. As care workers we must value and respect their ability to retain as much control as possible.

You can demonstrate respect in the following ways:

- listen actively to what the person is expressing
- acknowledge what they have expressed
- value what they say
- deliver care in line with their wishes
- have a collaborative approach to care.

Choice

Dementia affects several parts of the brain, including the part that is responsible for language. If no thought is given about how to encourage communication, choices may be made for the person because it is difficult to engage with them. When choices are always made for that person they can start to feel powerless and unable to make any decisions independently.

What you can do to promote choice for a person with dementia:

- understand the person's communication needs
- do not make assumptions about what they want
- provide people with information so they can make more informed choices.

Independence

It is essential to keep focused on people's strengths. Helping a person with dementia to have a level of control over their lives can give an enormous sense of autonomy and esteem. This may be simply taking part in washing their own face when carrying out personal care or pulling up their tights when getting dressed. Often people with dementia are not provided with adequate opportunity to promote their independence.

person-centred

care that is suited to an individual and their particular needs

How do you feel when you are not respected?

What you can do to promote independence:

- carry out an assessment of the person with dementia, including their strengths and abilities
- create a care plan that gives details of the person's abilities
- allow enough time to support the person at a pace that suits them
- support their method of communication
- provide a prompt for them at each step of an activity in a way that they understand, for example visual prompts.

Privacy

Once people develop dementia they often need to have people around to support them. This means their personal space is frequently invaded – often at intimate times. The need for additional support increases with the dementia. When the individual needs a level of support that cannot be provided at home they may need to move into a home – a communal space. After living all their life in a private home they now have to share their space with other people.

There are things that you can do to promote privacy:

- consider a person's culture/wishes and how this impacts on their privacy. For example, they may prefer same sex carers for personal care
- always knock before entering a room
- consider how the individual is feeling when carrying out personal care and ensure that the environment is private
- do not be persistent in discussing aspects of their life/past where they have demonstrated that they do not want to share this information with you
- respect all issues of personal confidentiality as appropriate
- be alert to behaviours that may be saying 'you are not respecting my privacy'.

Think carefully about your own experiences. What are the consequences of overriding someone's rights, both for you and the person with dementia?

If a person with dementia is denied basic rights, they may become withdrawn, suspicious or agitated. These behaviours may be a direct result of the way that the person is treated, *not* because of their dementia. If their rights are always denied the person withdraws further – accelerating their inability to maintain a level of independence and control. This decline could be a direct consequence of the type of care that you provide.

Helping a person with dementia to make decisions about their care

A person with dementia may have difficulty making some choices without help. However, the impact that dementia has varies enormously between people. Some may have very good insight into their condition whereas others may deny or not recognise that they need any support at all. Remember that if the individual is unable to make certain decisions it should not be assumed that they are unable to make *any* decisions about their care.

The type of support that you could offer a person to enable them to make choices includes:

- giving them clear information about the choices that are available to them
- providing information about choices in context (in the environment where the activity is going to take place)
- making sure that this information is delivered in a way that the person can understand
- monitoring their response and getting feedback on the care that is delivered
- choosing a time of day when they are more receptive because of their fluctuating states or the impact of certain medications
- arranging the environment in a way that helps better communication.

It is important to get a balance between the person's rights to make choices that may put them at risk and your duty of care. Sometimes it can be difficult to uphold a person's choices and this may cause conflict and concern about the risk to them. It may be that a person with dementia is trying to communicate something through their behaviour that they are not able to explain to you.

1. The person might be feeling unsafe or that they do not have control over the situation.
2. There might be an underlying reason for their behaviour. The person could be in pain when they are moving but not be able to express this.

Have you ever been faced with a situation where a person with dementia chooses not to eat their food or take their medication? What did you do?

3. Someone who is refusing to eat might be feeling depressed and have lost their appetite, or they may be finding it difficult to swallow food.

4. You might have asked the person to do something in a different way, which is causing them confusion.

5. The individual may find the different noises in the room too difficult to process at once and this may be creating a sense of frustration.

You must always balance your responsibilities to provide a safe environment with the individual's rights and wishes to take risks.

Activity 5

Pick one of the scenarios detailed in the numbered list on page 10 and above. Write the number here [ ]. What would you do in this situation?

_____

_____

What further action is required?

_____

_____

An unnecessary level of support can lead to loss of power and control

Action to take where a person is unable to make informed choices

This section helps you identify where the person with dementia is unable to make choices because of their impairment. The Mental Capacity Act 2005 states that a person with dementia is at first assumed to have **capacity**. A person who has been assessed as having capacity by the appropriate professional must be enabled to make their own choices, regardless of whether these put them at risk. The choices that people make will be influenced by their personality and experience but will also be made on the basis of their ability to understand the consequences of that choice.

The difficulty faced by care professionals is to understand if an individual's decision is an informed one (i.e. the consequences of the choice are understood) or if the decision has been made based on a limited ability to understand the risks. Just because someone has a diagnosis of dementia does not mean that they are unable to make choices. A person with dementia may be able to make an informed choice about one thing but cannot do this about another. Therefore a capacity assessment must be based on individual decisions and should not make assumptions.

Deciding if a person is at risk and how, should be completed jointly with a supervisor and may involve more specialist input from other people, such as:

- occupational therapist
- dietician
- doctor
- psycho-geriatrician
- nurse
- physiotherapist
- speech and language therapist
- social worker
- members of the person's family.

capacity

the ability to make informed decisions

Choices only become a concern for the carer where they pose a risk to the person. Your role is not only to support the person to make a choice where this is possible, but also to maintain their safety. Therefore it is important to understand risks.

Care scenario: Amy

Amy has dementia and lives in a residential home. In the mornings Amy has always been able to get out of bed and get dressed with some minimal support and then walk independently down to the dining area where she has chosen to have breakfast. Over the past week Amy has been staying in bed longer and longer; she is reluctant to get up in the morning and does not do very much for herself when getting dressed. Her mobility has reduced also and she has started to get pressure sores. Amy's appetite has also become very poor and she usually only eats a few spoonfuls of her food. When carers encourage her to eat more she refuses.

1. Has Amy got the right to refuse her food?
2. What are the risks?
3. What professionals could help you to understand the risks better?

It should only be necessary to override an individual's rights if it has been established (by the appropriate professionals) that the person is unable to make informed decisions as a result of their dementia. You alone *cannot* and *must not* make that decision, as this could be deemed as abuse. The Mental Capacity Act 2005 was drawn up to outline the processes of supporting people to make decisions where there is a question about their capacity to make choices (see also page 92).

Mental Capacity Act 2005

The main principles of the act are:

- *All people are presumed to have capacity until it is proved that they do not.*

- *A person must not be treated as unable to make a decision until all practical steps to help them do so have been taken.*

- *A person should not be treated as unable to make a decision because they make an unwise decision.*

- *A decision made under the act has to be done so in the person's 'best interest'.*

- *Before a person's rights are overridden thought must be given as to how this can be done in the least restrictive way possible.*

The importance of developing a person-to-person relationship

This section looks at how to form relationships with people with dementia and how important this is to working in a person-centred way.

Developing relationships

There have been many medical advances in the field of dementia yet the most effective interventions first need a trusting relationship and are based on the social model of care.

Health and disease can be affected by internal and external factors. This idea is demonstrated in the medical model of care (internal factors that affect the individual) and the social model of care (external factors that affect the individual).

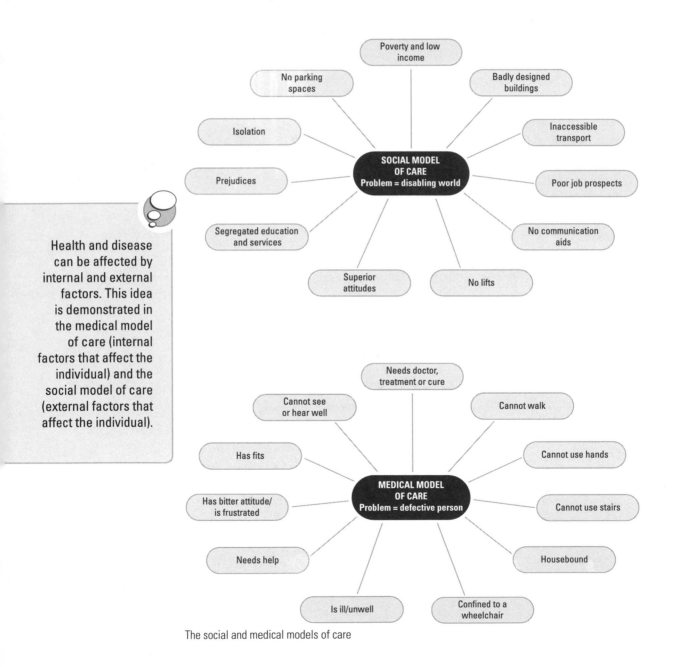

The social and medical models of care

The social model shows how the difficulties experienced by the person with dementia are made worse by other factors that are beyond their control, such as negative relationships. A negative relationship will undermine a person by taking away their independence. Sometimes, without even realising it, carers can make things much worse for the person with dementia.

There are certain important things we can do to influence both negatively and positively the effect the dementia has on the person. Negative behaviours can undermine the person and further confuse them.

Examples of negative behaviour include:

- doing something for people when they can do it themselves
- keeping people in their room without adequate social interaction
- treating the person as an object
- intimidating the person by using physical or verbal threats, whether these are subtle or explicit
- invalidating people's thoughts and feelings
- undermining their right to personal choice.

Tom Kitwood developed the idea that our behaviour may have a negative impact on the person with dementia and may even make their mental state worse by deskilling and devaluing them.

Within a relationship your role as a carer is to provide:

- warmth and respect
- safety and security
- independence and inclusion.

Our behaviour towards a person with dementia may be affected by assumptions or stereotypes that we hold. One of these stereotypes may be that the person is a 'powerless', passive recipient of care. This can lead to the carer developing a power base where care is provided *to* and not *with* the person with dementia.

The carer needs to build skills to develop a relationship that enables the person with dementia to feel secure and valued, and gives them a sense of identity and control. This can have a very positive impact on the person's ability to cope with the condition.

Have you ever carried out any of the negative behaviours listed opposite, either to make things easier for yourself or to save time? What could you have done differently?

It is important always to take into account the difficulties experienced by a person with dementia and to maximise their strengths.

1. What factors are important in developing relationships?

2. What can you do to support the process?

The following factors are important in developing positive relationships.

Communication

Communication forms the basis of a relationship. In the care plan there will be details of how the person with dementia communicates. If an individual finds it difficult to understand you or to express themselves, you should try to overcome this, for example by providing any aids that are needed.

Empathy

It is important that you have a good understanding of the issues that the person with dementia is facing. The experience of loss of control can be overwhelming. You should demonstrate through your behaviour that you have some understanding of the individual's feelings and emotions.

Trust

The person with dementia relies heavily on the support received, as the dementia makes the person vulnerable. They need a relationship where the carer will value them – regardless of their lack of abilities – and support them to promote their strengths and maximise their independence.

Care scenario: Mary

Mary has dementia of the Alzheimer's type. She has been living in residential care for the last two years. The Alzheimer's has caused her to have impairments in her language, memory, concentration and coordination skills. When supporting Mary to get dressed, she will often talk quickly and forcefully in a distressed manner. The content of the language varies and usually does not make sense to the carer. However, the manner in which Mary relates this information is always the same – quick, forceful and distressed.

1. What are the feelings underlying Mary's behaviour?
2. How can the carer help change Mary's behaviour?
3. What is Mary experiencing?
4. How can you demonstrate that you understand what she is going through?
5. How could you gain her trust?

The following can stop us from forming positive relationships with the people we care for:

- fear
- our assumptions
- lack of common ground with the other person
- difficulty in engaging with the person
- pressures of work
- working for short periods of time, e.g. as an agency worker.

Activity 6

Complete the following table.

Barriers to relationships	How can we overcome these
Fear	
Our assumptions	
Lack of common ground with the other person	
Difficulty in engaging with the person	
Pressures of work	
Working for short periods of time, e.g. as an agency worker	

1. What else stops us from forming positive relationships?
2. Using the table above, write an action plan for developing a relationship with someone in your care.

How loss and change are commonly experienced by people with dementia

People with dementia have to deal with loss and subsequent change. This section helps you to think about the losses that are typically faced by the person with dementia and how this requires them to adapt and change.

People with dementia have to cope with:

- psychological losses
- physical losses
- social losses.

All of us experience loss and change in our lives at different times and have to deal with this. If we can understand this we are better able to relate to the experiences of others.

Think of a time when you have lost something or someone.

How did you feel? Over what period of time did this affect you? Did change come from this? What personal resources could you draw on to help you understand this? What kind of support did others give you?

Activity 7

Look at the diagram below and try to add some of your own examples of losses.

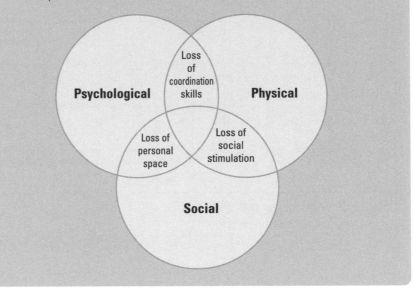

Loss can be simple or significant. We can usually deal with simple losses, such as losing our keys, relatively easily. However, the individual with dementia is unable to draw on personal skills to deal with this, such as tracing their steps back in a logical order to find where they last had their keys. This is because they have lost the ability to sequence their thoughts and actions. Therefore the experience of simple loss for them is profound.

When we consider dealing with significant loss the impact is greater. For a person with dementia this may include loss of:

- a partner or a much-loved pet
- a home and their own personal space
- occupation
- contact with friends
- physical and mental abilities, which dramatically change functioning.

Many of these losses can occur together, with devastating effect.

Dealing with loss

There is a recognised process which a person has to go through when dealing with loss or grief and change. These stages are listed below.

- Shock and denial – when someone starts to understand that they are losing their mental abilities they may deny this with **confabulation** or by refusing to admit that there is a problem.
- Anger – the person with dementia may start to experience anger due to their loss of control
- Rationalisation – the individual may find it more difficult to make sense of their situation as a result of their dementia
- Acceptance – the person begins to adapt and changes take place to compensate for the loss.

confabulation
creating imaginary experiences to make up for loss of memory

Care scenario: John

John has recently been diagnosed with dementia. During the last few months his ability to care for himself has reduced significantly. Home carers were provided at first to support with personal care in the mornings, but John soon needed help with other activities of daily living and the carers were then attending to him three times a day. Concern grew about his safety during the day and he was therefore referred to a day centre. One night his neighbour called as he had found him outside in his bed clothes. John's family suggested to him that he might need to go to a residential home. John was very angry at this suggestion, stating that he was clearly able to look after himself. But John was then admitted to hospital and from there was placed in a residential home.

1. What are the losses that John has faced?
2. Can you identify the stages of loss involved?

Dealing with change

There are certain things that you can do to support a person with dementia who is having to deal with change. For example, you can:

- offer the opportunity to discuss and build on the changes
- draw on strengths to minimise the losses experienced by the person.

The table below gives some real-life examples.

Example	Action
Loss of garden	Offer a role helping with the gardening in the residential setting
Loss of status and self-esteem	Valuing the individual, acknowledging their strengths

However, we may also influence the losses negatively by emphasising or reaffirming them and by not making the most of people's strengths.

When someone with dementia is not allowed to take part in activities of daily living (e.g. washing, dressing, eating a meal), it can make their experience of loss worse. This is not only because of their dementia, but also because they can't do some things because someone does it for them. Imagine how you might feel if a person caring for you tried to help you get dressed very fast. This would mean that you are unable to take part in the activity and may also feel confused. In addition, if the feelings of a person with dementia are continually dismissed as 'nonsense' or 'being silly', their sense of loss will also be increased.

Experiences like those described above are very common for individuals with dementia. If you always 'take over', this can cause someone to have little faith in their own abilities, leading to a low self-esteem and a feeling of **disempowerment**. A person with dementia will often become less motivated to do things for themselves and to express themselves.

As you can see, through our actions, we may unintentionally cause a person with dementia to become withdrawn and, eventually, to be in a vegetative state. The experience of loss, from diagnosis to death, can therefore be very great and it is possible to do more harm than good if you take too much control. It is therefore very important to make sure that the services we provide to people with dementia are appropriate and do not make the feeling of loss worse.

Some losses may also occur as a result of age, or other physical or mental difficulties.

disempowerment
the feeling that you have no power or control over what happens to you

Think of a person with dementia who you work with. What losses do you think they have experienced as a result of their dementia? What can you do to reduce their feelings of loss?

The importance of having a good understanding of the person's needs

This section helps you understand the importance of completing up-to-date assessments. This is so you can provide care in a way that will respond to the rapidly changing needs of people with dementia. The assessment is the foundation of the care plan and will need to be reviewed frequently. The assessment process is shown below.

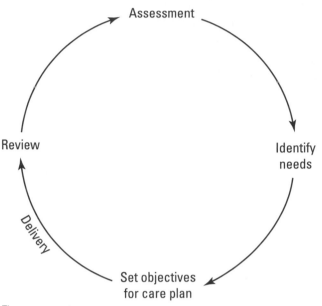

The assessment process

Assessments/reviews will be required:

- where there is a change in a person's physical or mental health
- if a person with dementia requests an assessment
- to review a case periodically
- when a review is requested by significant others, for example external agencies such as social services.

Assessments

When completing assessments remember that a person may not have the same perception of their needs as others, such as care workers or their family.

A person-centred approach to care is a way of putting the person at the centre of the process by ensuring that:

- the needs and wishes of the person with dementia are clearly defined
- the individual has a sense of control in the planning and development of their care
- the individual's strengths are used to promote independence.

When we carry out assessments it is important to use techniques that enable a person with dementia to be as involved as possible. If we have a good understanding of an individual's history we are able to provide care in a way that reinforces their identity and makes the most of their strengths. It may also help us to understand messages in their behaviour, which can further help in their care.

The process of getting to know about the life of a person with dementia can be a positive and stimulating experience for that person. For example, if the individual is no longer able to write or read, pictures can be used to stimulate thought or tell a story. This activity is commonly known as life story work and is used frequently in the care of people with dementia. It can help to:

- promote inclusion (make them feel involved)
- encourage mental stimulation
- improve communication
- support the development of a positive relationship.

Throughout the process it is important that you:

- use active listening skills, such as having eye contact with the person with dementia
- validate what the individual says
- support the recording of the story.

In completing this process you are able to build a relationship with the person that is based on respect of their past and an understanding of how this has an impact on their current needs.

Care scenario: Rachel

Rachel has lived in nursing care for the last six months. She was diagnosed with a multi-infarct dementia about three years ago. Very little is known about her life because she has limited communication. Sometimes she gets her words mixed up. She does not understand written words, but has a good grasp of pictures. Her room is full of pictures of the past and in one picture she is wearing a uniform. Rachel has a poor short-term memory and may forget recent events, and at times this distresses her. Rachel needs to wear a hearing aid but has excellent eyesight. Rachel's family live far away and can't visit very often.

1. What steps would you take to build up a picture of Rachel's life?
2. What techniques would you use to support her inclusion in the process of assessment?

Activity 8

Complete the table below. An example has been provided for you.

Which people could give you information to support your assessment?	What type of information could you get from them?
Doctor	Medical history

How to involve people in the planning of their care

A person with dementia will often have a different view from the professionals about the care and support that they need. It is important to establish their point of view on the support that is required as it will affect how you plan their care. Below is an extract from a care plan for a person with dementia called Ronald.

Area of care: Individual's assessment:	Nutrition When Ronald is offered meals he says 'What is it?' If he likes it he says 'Leave it there'; if he does not he says 'Leave me alone'. Ronald eats very slowly and if disturbed he becomes agitated and states 'Don't rush me'.
Key worker's assessment:	Ronald has been observed refusing his meals. The dietician has been involved and has recommended pureed meals but Ronald refused to eat these. This has been reviewed and his diet now consists of soft foods and *Ensure* (nutritional drink). Ronald needs direct supervision and prompting at mealtimes.
Area of care: Individual's assessment:	Personal hygiene Ronald feels that he can look after himself and therefore does not need any help in this area.
Key worker's assessment:	Ronald needs assistance and encouragement to have a bath. This should be approached sensitively.
Area of care: Individual's assessment:	Incontinence Ronald says 'There is nothing wrong with me' or 'Why are you changing that?' and protests. If he has been incontinent he thinks that someone else has put it there.
Key worker's assessment:	Ronald is doubly incontinent. He requires a hoist to manoeuvre him onto the commode. A pad is required to manage incontinence. Ronald is a very private person and can become embarrassed easily, and thinks that he should be left alone. Ronald is prone to a urinary tract infection and therefore this needs to be monitored effectively.

What actions could be placed in the care plan under the headings below which would take account of Ronald's perception of his need? An example has been included.

Area of need	Action
Incontinence	When supervising Ronald on the commode, this should be done discreetly.
Personal hygiene	
Nutrition	

Strengths-based assessment

Your assessment of an individual should not be focused just on physical needs, such as needing support with personal care and feeding. You should also include the social, emotional, spiritual and cultural areas of care. Traditional care plans have been too focused on problems and have tended to look more at problem-solving than at a person's strengths. There is now growing evidence that a strengths-based approach to the care of people with dementia is more effective. We are beginning to recognise that there is much that we can do to improve the quality of care for people with dementia.

When we think about strengths it is important to think about the things that we take for granted. These can include the ability to walk independently, to recognise objects, to be involved in some level with activities of daily living, to retain memories of the past or even the ability to laugh.

Look at a care plan. Is there detail in the care plan of the person's strengths? Is it clearly outlined how these can be promoted?

Activity 9

Think of a person with dementia that you know and write down some of their strengths. In the next column, write how you can make the most of these strengths in the care that you provide, particularly how you can encourage the individual to use their strengths to make the most of their weaknesses.

Strengths	How can you make the most of those strengths?

How will focusing on strengths in your assessments change the way that you work with a person with dementia?

In this section you are going to learn about the importance of working with families and friends of the individual with dementia in a supportive and educative role.

Providing information to family carers about person-centred care

The impact of dementia on family life can be devastating. The condition may not only influence the structure of day-to-day life but also reshape family relationships.

A quote from a family member living with someone with dementia:

'Sometimes it feels like living with a stranger, a shadow. When I look deep into her eyes I can see her, feel her. Sometimes I get exhausted and angry, but if she's not here I miss her.'

Have you experienced having a family member with dementia? What do you remember about the experience? What helped the situation?

A person with dementia can require almost continuous support and so the informal carer is often left feeling both physically and emotionally exhausted. You can help informal carers and family members by providing them with information. This will develop their understanding of person-centred care which will improve the experience both for the person with dementia as well as the informal carer.

Person-centred care to family members

This approach to care:

- focuses on the whole person and their world not just the diseased brain
- focuses on strengths not weaknesses and so aims to maintain independence
- values the views and perspectives of the person with dementia, encouraging their involvement in the planning of services
- recognises people's uniqueness and individuality
- recognises the person within the context of the outside world and their relationships.

It is important that we do not make assumptions about family or friend relationships. You should take care when you discuss a situation with family members. Has the individual given you permission to talk to them?

Family members are an invaluable source of information as they usually have a good understanding of the individual's current and previous wishes. It is important that you listen to their views and make them feel supported.

Support networks/organisations available to support people with dementia

The help that services offer can assist in reducing some of the day-to-day challenges faced by informal carers. But the process of getting help from support services can be lengthy, complex and frustrating. Then, when they have got the service in place, the experience for informal carers can be intrusive and difficult. If you have knowledge about services, you can be of valuable support to informal carers.

Support services available

Services can include the following:

- The Alzheimer's Society has local support networks available that can provide opportunities to talk to other people in a similar position. Their website can provide factsheets full of practical advice on how to support the person with dementia. A link to this website has been made available at www.heinemann.co.uk/hotlinks by entering the express code 2307P.

- Most areas also have a carers group which can offer advice on access to services, including how to go about getting financial support.

- The individual's GP will be able to refer them to counselling services.

- The social services team will be able to provide practical support such as respite services, day care and home care.

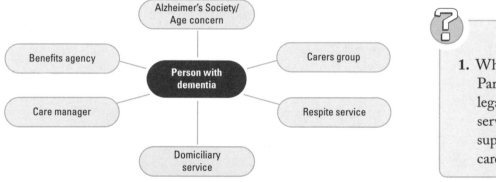

The range of services available for people with dementia

What are the contact details for your local carers group?

What are the contact details for your local Alzheimer's group?

What is the telephone number for your local social services department?

1. Which Act of Parliament gives a legal duty to local services to provide support to informal carers?

Care scenario: Maria

Maria's mother was recently diagnosed with Alzheimer's disease. Maria works full time and is finding it difficult to provide the practical support her mother needs. As her mother can no longer carry out domestic tasks Maria has to do the shopping and the housework. She is also cooking and freezing meals, but her mother is now finding it difficult to manage the microwave. Maria's mother has been reluctant to accept help from neighbours and friends. Maria's relationship with her partner is becoming strained because of the time that she has to devote to her mother.

1. Who would you advise Maria goes to see?

In this section you are going to learn about the measures you can use to prevent harm to people with dementia.

What you need to learn

- Why it is important to have an awareness of abuse.
- How to involve family and friends in safeguarding adults.
- The role of independent advocacy in safeguarding adults.
- The assistive technologies available to minimise risks.
- The effect of the environment.
- Why there is an increased risk of falls.

Why it is important to have an awareness of abuse

abuse

intentional acts or omissions of care which lead to harm of a vulnerable person

People with dementia are at more risk of **abuse** than other members of society. This is because of failing mental and often physical abilities. These concerns were highlighted in an important report, No Secrets 2000. The report acknowledged that abuse was widespread, and took place within different settings. The most common place was in the home and the second most common was in a residential setting. The report called for a multi-agency approach to tackling abuse and required all care workers to undertake training in this area.

In order to work with people with dementia you need to understand:

- the types of abuse
- the signs and symptoms of this abuse
- how to prevent abuse
- how to report abuse
- how to deal with disclosure
- the role of the legal framework.

The types of abuse are:

- physical
- sexual
- racial
- emotional
- financial
- institutional
- neglect
- chemical.

Activity 10

Think of the signs of the different types of abuse that you might see and write them in the table below.

Types of abuse	Signs
Physical	
Sexual	
Racist	
Emotional	
Financial	
Institutional	
Neglect	
Chemical	

What is the procedure for whistle blowing in your organisation?

What is the role of the General Social Care Council in administering the Protection of Vulnerable Adults Register?

There are different reasons why people might be abused. It may take place because of:

- poor understanding of an individual's needs and abilities
- poor understanding of aggression as a form of communication
- stress experienced by informal carers
- power structures in organisations
- lack of organisational support and training.

Activity 11

Consider now some solutions that might prevent abuse occurring as a result of one of the triggers listed above. Write them in the table below.

Causes of abuse	Possible solutions
Poor understanding of individual's needs	
Poor understanding of aggression	
Stress of informal carers	
Power structures	
Lack of organisational support/training	

People with dementia may commonly be abused through over-medication to control or manage their behaviours, or by being kept informally in institutions against their will.

How to involve family and friends in safeguarding adults

The importance of choice

In the earlier stages of dementia the individual is often supported by informal carers who may need advice on how to keep their family member or friend safe.

Informal carers can find it difficult to allow a person with dementia to make choices and take risks for themselves because of an over-concern for their safety. Your role is to ensure that they get advice about safety measures but also to encourage the informal carer to allow the individual to have some control over their decisions and actions.

Informal carers can tell you a lot about their family member or friend and you need to work in partnership with them to provide a safe and enabling environment for the person with dementia. You can jointly agree how you can deliver the care between you. You might need to provide additional support to informal carers that you work with because they may be elderly or not have English as their first language.

You are likely to have more contact with informal carers if you are supporting someone in their own home. However, if you are working in a residential setting the family and friends of the person are still likely to want to be involved in some decisions. If you have concerns about safety make sure that you raise them with your line manager, the individual and the informal carer and document them clearly. Concerns may also be raised as part of a formal review of the care plan. Any safety measures should fit in with existing routines, religious beliefs, cultural identity and social needs.

A number of factsheets are available which can provide step-by-step guidance about providing a safe environment. Other professionals will also have an essential role in advising on how to make an environment safe. An occupational therapist may be able to provide aids to promote independence and reduce risks. A physiotherapist may be able to provide advice and guidance on mobility equipment and how this can be used safely.

The role of independent advocacy in safeguarding adults

An individual that you work with might already have an advocate. An advocate is an independent person who works alongside an individual to help them get their views across. It is important to understand a person's views in order to provide better care.

Advocates are detached from the situation and therefore cannot be influenced by opposing interests. Advocates do not make decisions for people, or give guidance, but instead their role is to represent people's views, wishes and rights where they have difficulty speaking up for themselves.

The needs of people with dementia will vary according to the type and stage of the illness and so it is important to find an advocate who has the correct skills. The advocate should be able to develop a good relationship with the individual.

There are many reasons why a person with dementia may need an advocate:

- to identify wishes
- to understand risks better
- where there is a conflict between the individual and the informal carer
- where the person is unable to access a service
- where a professional feels that the person's expressed wishes have been influenced by others
- where a person's views may need to be clarified, particularly when a decision to move into residential care is required
- if the person has been 'sectioned' under the Mental Health Act 1983.

Obtain a factsheet from Age Concern or the Alzheimer's Society that gives advice to informal carers on making an environment safe. You could research this on their websites.

What does the factsheet say?

Minimum Standards – Commission of Social Care Inspectorate

OUTCOME: Service users' legal rights are protected.

STANDARD 17.2: If a service user lacks capacity to make informed decisions they have to be provided with an advocate.

Care scenario: Paula

Paula has been diagnosed with dementia in the last year. She has been going out less as she becomes anxious when she is out. She now requires more support with most activities of daily living. Paula's daughter, Jane, is concerned about her mother's safety and well-being in the community. Jane has talked to Paula about this. Paula does not want to move from home but is concerned about upsetting her daughter and becoming a burden to her. Paula reluctantly agrees to go to social services with Jane to discuss this.

1. What is the danger of asking Jane about Paula's wishes?
2. How might Paula and Jane represent the risks differently?
3. What might Paula tell an independent advocate that she would not tell Jane?
4. What are the benefits to Paula of having an independent advocate?

The assistive technologies available to minimise risks

An assistive technology is a product or service which enables the person with dementia to be more independent or to live in a safer environment (examples are shown in Activity 12).

Benefits

These technologies enable the individual to use their remaining strengths which can improve their quality of life and make them feel in more control.

Assistive technologies can delay or prevent admission to care homes.

Key points in using assistive technologies

It is important to remember the following key points:

- not all products suit all people
- some people might find it difficult to adapt to the use of assistive technologies
- an assessment may need to be completed by an occupational therapist
- only some equipment can be provided by the local authority; equipment purchased privately might be expensive.

How can you make a referral to occupational therapy in your local area?

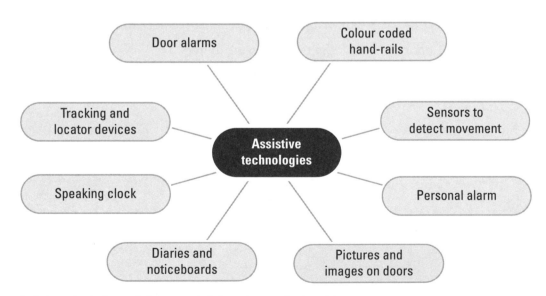

Assistive technologies can help to promote independence and reduce risk

Activity 12

Assistive technologies have two main purposes: to promote independence and reduce risks. In the table below, fill in the empty boxes showing how each device can promote independence or reduce risks (or both).

Assistive technology	Purpose	Promotes independence	Reduces risks
Medication aids	Blister packs and dosset boxes put the medication in day and time order which can remind the person to take their medication		
Sensors that detect movement	A sensor mat can be placed next to the bed to alert a carer that the person has got up. They can also be placed on a chair which might alert the carer that they have been gone for long periods		
Sensors that detect water, gas and heat	Sensors can be discreetly placed to detect floods, gas and high temperatures		
Sensors that detect falls	Sensors can be placed on the person that can detect the impact of falls		
Personal pendant alarms	These alert staff/carers in an emergency		
Pictures and images on doors	These can help people to find their way around and into their own room		
Notice boards	Can be used to prompt memory		
Speaking clocks	Can be used to remind the person of the date and time		
Tracking devices	These show where people are when outside, but may only work when within a certain range		
Locator devices	These are attached to something that might be frequently lost, such as keys		
Recorded messages	These are used to prompt memory, such as when you leave the house, 'Don't forget your keys'		
Door alarms	These could be linked to a monitoring system so would alert carers that the person has exited the building		
Colour-coded handrails	These aid vision and provide support with transfers		

The effect of the environment

Poor environment

A poor environment can have an extreme impact on the quality of life for a person with dementia, affecting their safety and independence.

Someone with dementia may have particular difficulty moving around their environment. This is because of changes in the brain that cause problems in the way they see things and/or their coordination. If you do not understand this, you could be creating an environment that will cause emotional difficulty, challenging behaviour, increased confusion, and also increased risk of falls and loss of independence.

The brain of a person with dementia may interpret things differently from you, for example they might mistake patterns for steps, which can lead to falls. Patterns in carpets can be mistaken for faces and this can be frightening. Down-lighting can cause shadows which can further confuse the person. They may find it difficult to distinguish an object from its background.

A poor short-term memory can lead to people getting lost; for example, a common difficulty is incontinence because they are unable to find the toilet. You can make sure that measures are taken to assist them in finding the toilet, such as colour-coded arrows. Certain colours may stay in the memory for longer and can therefore be used to remind an individual of where they are.

In the early stages of dementia changes to the home environment, such as moving furniture around, can lead to complete disorientation. It is important to keep the environment the same, but make it safe.

In the later stages of dementia the individual may not recognise themselves in the mirror, and looking into a mirror can cause fear. If a person is experiencing this problem it may be better to remove all mirrors.

Ways of improving the environment

You can:

- make sure that the environment is clutter free
- use assistive technologies
- eliminate patterns in the carpet
- use lighting that does not create shadows
- ensure that there is plenty of open space, including space to go out in the garden
- make sure not to move furniture around in the environment.

The main objective is to ensure that the person is safe yet has as much control as possible.

Look around the environment where you work. Try to think of three things that you could do to make it better for people with dementia.

Why there is an increased risk of falls

Older people with dementia are twice as likely to have a fall as an older person without dementia. Most people with dementia are older and so have fragile bones which are more likely to suffer a fracture if they have a fall. Recovery from a fracture can be difficult when a person also has dementia.

What increases the risk?

People with a dementia of the Lewy Body type (see page 84) may be more at risk. This is because of the way that the dementia can create difficulties in walking, often known as a shuffling **gait.** There are also other factors – sometimes more than one at a time for the individual.

Medication

There are several ways that medication may increase the risk of falls; for example, some types of medication can influence balance while others may make the person drowsy.

Poor coordination and instability

The dementia may affect the brain in a way that influences the way people see spaces or how they manage their balance. This causes an unsteady gait. The dementia may also affect the individual's ability to follow a sequence of actions, which means they might stop halfway and fall.

Poor environment

As discussed on page 34, a poor environment can cause many problems for the person with dementia. Obstacles that are difficult to move around can cause great difficulty and people with dementia may perceive the environment differently.

Dizziness

Changes in blood pressure can lead to dizziness which increases the risk of falls. This may be more common in certain types of dementia, such as vascular dementia (see page 83).

Bone degeneration

Problems associated with the degeneration of the bones in older age may increase the risk of falls. Pain caused by arthritis can create further risks.

Eyesight

Poor eyesight can obviously cause difficulties and lead to increased risk of falls. There is a general deterioration in eyesight with older age.

Agitation

Behaviour such as wandering and agitation may cause rapid and sudden movements, so increasing the risk of falls.

Find out about the Minimum Standards for Care Homes Section 19–28.

gait
the way a person walks

Reporting falls

If a person with dementia has a fall, it is important to write a detailed report of the incident. This will give you valuable information on the prevention of future accidents. You should try to break your report down and consider the period before, during and after the incident. Think about how the individual, other people and the environment interacted.

Activity 13

Think about a time when someone has fallen when you were on duty. What action did you take? Write this up in the following way:

	Before	During	After
Environment			
Individual			
Other people			

Minimising the risk of falls

A physiotherapist will be able to offer advice and support on how to minimise the risk of falls and what mobility aids could be used.

You can also take some measures to minimise the risks of falls. These include the following:

- consider how the environment can be changed to make it safer
- talk to the doctor if you are concerned that medication may be influencing the person's balance
- follow any physiotherapy guidelines that support the care plan
- if dizziness is a worry, refer to the doctor or, if there are nurses within your organisation, report it to them
- use all aids and adaptations that have been provided. If you are concerned about whether they are appropriate, talk to your senior or local occupational therapist
- when falls occur, note down carefully and clearly what happened before, during and after, as this can help build up a picture of the causes
- if the person with dementia wears a hip protector regularly make sure that this is in place
- look at the individual's footwear to make sure that it is appropriate.

Consequences of falls

Many people with dementia are placed in residential care because not enough is done to minimise the risk of falls. Poor funding in elderly care may mean that community services cannot adequately support the risks of falls and other problems. For the person with dementia this is a high and unnecessary price to pay and can lead to further problems for them. More informed services are able to minimise risks by working in partnership with the individuals involved and other support services, and so keep people in their own homes and in the community.

Much can be done to lessen the risk of falls for a person with dementia

In this section you will learn about meeting an individual's nutritional needs and the consequences of poor nutrition, hygiene and exercise.

What you need to learn

- The nutritional needs of people with dementia.
- Encouraging exercise for people with dementia.
- Ensuring good personal care for people with dementia.
- Living in a clean and enabling environment.

The nutritional needs of people with dementia

This section covers the importance of maintaining a good balanced diet, including the consequences of poor nutrition and why people with dementia may have problems in this area.

A person with dementia needs to eat a good balanced diet to ensure the best physical state. Good nutrition can prevent infections, pressure sores and other skin problems, improve concentration and improve general well-being.

Problems with nutrition

If a person with dementia starts to develop problems with feeding it can lead rapidly to **malnutrition**.

malnutrition

insufficient nutrition; where there is not the right food necessary for health

Physical changes in the brain may result in the individual experiencing some changes in their abilities. This may include their memory, language, concentration and motivation, which can affect their nutrition. For example a person may lack the motivation to eat, or in the later stages might lose the coordination skills to feed themselves or develop problems swallowing. They may forget whether they have eaten, or that they need to eat at all. A person with dementia may lose the ability to concentrate on the activity of cooking or eating long enough to complete it. They may experience changes in their taste sensations. In advanced cases individuals may require feeding tubes in order to meet their nutritional needs.

A person with dementia often develops depression when they have an insight into their deteriorating functions. Depression can then lead to loss of interest in food and general reduced appetite. However, depression can be treated and if concerned a referral should be made to a GP.

Lack of activity can cause other physical problems, including constipation. It is important to increase fibre and fluid intake in the diet in order to avoid constipation.

Poor oral health can lead to problems with eating. Some medications can also affect appetite and behaviour and should be considered if eating is a difficulty.

Behavioural difficulties that are caused by changes in the brain may lead to difficulties in eating; these can include wandering, where an individual will not sit for long enough to eat their food.

Malnutrition and other physical problems can lead to dementia-like symptoms, sometimes known as **confusional states**. For example, some infections can lead to increased confusion and some may also lead to agitation.

As dementia affects the language functions in the brain, the individual may be unable to tell you if they are hungry or in pain. It is important to be observant and keep records. Input and output charts may be used to monitor a person's nutritional status if they are not well, for example being sick.

What you can do

There are certain things that you can do to help with a person's nutrition.

- Seek advice from a dietician if you are worried about nutritional status.
- Remind individuals if they find it hard to remember about drinking and eating.
- Ensure that the person with dementia is involved as much as possible in the preparation of meals and feeding themselves.
- Arrange food attractively on a plate and keep it warm.
- Prepare simple foods that can be eaten without a lot of coordination skills.
- Ensure that the texture of the food is appropriate for the person; where necessary seek advice from a speech and language therapist.
- Try to cater for the changes in taste that are sometimes experienced because of the physical changes in the brain.
- Supervise mealtimes to ensure that the person does eat; it may be necessary to provide additional support.
- Use appropriate aids that can support people with coordination difficulties when they are eating. Where necessary seek advice from an occupational therapist.
- Consult the GP if you are concerned about infections.

confusional state

a temporary condition caused by some sort of infection

Activity 14

Complete the table below for a person with dementia that you know and then make recommendations at the end to incorporate into the care plan.

Question	✔ or X	Question	✔ or X
Is the individual able to express food preferences?		Does the individual show any behaviours that affect the process of eating?	
Is the individual able to express when they are hungry?		Does the individual suffer from coordination problems?	
Is the individual able to feed themselves independently?		Does the individual need any especially adapted equipment to enable them to eat?	
Does the individual have insight into what makes a balanced diet?		Are there any environmental factors that influence eating/feeding?	
Does the individual need prompting to eat?		Is the individual more alert at certain times of the day?	
Is the individual experiencing other physical problems that are affecting their nutritional state?		Does the individual have problems with their oral health that may lead to difficulties eating?	
Is the individual on any medication that affects their appetite?		Does the individual have problems with swallowing?	
Is the individual experiencing any mental health problems other than dementia that affect their nutritional state?		Does the individual have religious or cultural needs that affect their diet?	

- Based on the information above, what recommendations do you make for the care plan?
- Do you need to seek advice from other professionals? If so, which professional?

Encouraging exercise for people with dementia

This section looks at factors which influence lack of activity and the consequences of poor exercise.

Reasons for inactivity

These can include:

- lack of motivation
- difficulty judging spaces causing fear when moving around
- difficulty with coordination causing fear when moving around
- a disabling environment can increase fear and therefore limit mobility
- musculoskeletal problems associated with old age (however, not all individuals who have dementia will be old and therefore may not be affected by this difficulty).

Exercise may be required to regain some functions that are lost, for example after a stroke or after a hip replacement; this is called **rehabilitation**. However, many people with dementia find that rehabilitation takes longer because they have memory problems and may find it difficult to retain instructions, or they may not be able to understand the physiotherapist's instructions. The consequence of this is that the person with dementia becomes increasingly dependent and this may mean the difference between living at home or in a residential setting.

rehabilitation

to restore function to previous state

Additional support should be provided to prompt the individual who is unable to remember instructions for exercise.

Lack of exercise

Failure to exercise will lead to problems for all of us, but for the person with dementia it can mean:

- dependency; for example the person may lose their muscle strength and then their ability to walk
- muscle wastage and stiffness
- increased anxiety and stress
- an unsettled night – if a person exercises during the day they are likely to be more settled at night.

What you can do

There are certain things that you can do to help encourage exercise in people with dementia.

- Seek advice from a physiotherapist to ensure that the exercise is appropriate to each individual.
- Exercise need not be traditional; a meaningful activity that encourages gentle exercise can be used instead.
- Consider what other physical factors might influence exercise, such as poor sight or painful feet, and work to develop ways of overcoming these problems.
- Prompt individuals and encourage exercise; repeat instructions where necessary.
- Use appropriate communication techniques.
- Ensure that exercise has been incorporated into the care plan.

Exercise has many benefits for people with dementia

1. What are the benefits of exercise for the person with dementia?

Ensuring good personal care for people with dementia

Personal care is important in maintaining a healthy lifestyle. This section looks at the factors to consider when carrying out personal care for a person with dementia.

Problems with personal care

Poor personal hygiene can lead to:

- reduced social contact
- low self-esteem
- increased risk of infection.

Understand the need for sensitivity

Personal care is a very sensitive and individual concern. When supporting a person with dementia you need to consider their privacy and dignity. You must also try to promote their independence by enabling them to have as much control as possible over the activity. This is particularly important in dementia care because of the overwhelming loss of control that is experienced. It is obviously essential that personal care is provided in accordance with a person's religious and cultural beliefs and preferences.

It is important for you to identify what the individual's normal pattern of personal care is and not enforce personal care routines. If you are concerned that personal care is carried out so infrequently that it may lead to infections, the matter will need to be addressed with tact and sensitivity.

Good personal care should incorporate washing face, hands and body, and oral hygiene. When supporting someone with toileting, ensure that the individual is encouraged to wipe from front to back to reduce the risk of infection.

Signs of problems

Poor personal hygiene may be one of the initial indications of dementia. For example, the individual may be reluctant to let others know about their difficulties because they are embarrassed or frightened about what people will say. They may forget to change their clothes and will therefore wear the same clothes for several days.

Some people with dementia may be reluctant to have a bath or a shower because the process frightens them or they find it disorientating. Others may find it difficult because they lack sequencing skills as a result of the changes in the brain. For example, a woman might put her knickers on over her tights. It is important to specifically identify a person's difficulties and strengths in order to ensure that they can retain some control.

Some individuals may need to have more frequent personal care because of other physical problems. These can include incontinence and skin problems, such as pressure sores or scabies. If you do not provide adequate personal care there will be a risk of infection.

What you can do

There are some things that you can do to help with improving personal care.

- If people have sequencing problems, break down the activity into steps and prompt them through the process.
- Find out through sensitive discussion their preferences about personal care.
- Provide any appropriate aids to support their independence, such as grab rails.
- If a person is reluctant to wash, try to rephrase the way that you ask them.
- Ensure that infection control measures, such as gloves and aprons, are used to prevent the risk of infection.
- Encourage the individual to wash their hands before eating and after going to the toilet.
- Assisting people with the set-up – providing everything within easy reach – will enable them to be more independent.
- Allow plenty of time to carry out the activity.
- Consider safety measures when assisting someone with personal care, such as water temperature and the risk of slipping on wet floors.

Care scenario: Rasheed

Rasheed is 72 and lives at home with his wife. Before Rasheed suffered from dementia, he had always been very particular about his personal care, taking a regimental approach to showering and dressing on a daily basis. Recently his wife has started to notice that he lacks motivation during the day and has stopped washing. He has started to develop some skin problems. Every time Rasheed's wife talks to him about not showering he becomes angry and upset. In the next couple of months Rasheed develops a chest infection, and soon after he appears very confused and agitated. Rasheed starts to eat less and wants to stay in bed more.

1. What factors have influenced Rasheed's deterioration?
2. What action might be taken to solve some of the concerns?

Care scenario: Faridah

Faridah has dementia, a history of heart disease, diabetes and lives in a residential care home. Faridah also has some slight hearing problems, but she has a good sense of humour, good eyesight and is most comfortable spending time in her room which is very light and airy. Faridah has difficulty remembering instructions, and also has some coordination difficulties. Faridah is more able to understand things when they are presented in an uncomplicated way. When she talks, her sentences are often broken and short. Faridah is often reluctant to carry out personal care but has some skin problems that require the area to be kept clean. She is able to walk short distances but does get out of breath quickly. Faridah was born in Iran and, although she is not a practising Muslim, aspects of the faith are important to her.

Now consider Faridah's needs and how they can be supported. The first need has been completed for you. Try to consider how Faridah's rights affect the personal care process. What health and safety issues need to be considered? What are the risk factors regarding infections? It is also important to consider the communication factor in each personal care activity. This should be an important part of the care plan.

Need	How this will be supported
Faridah gets out of breath quickly	Ensure that the environment is set up to ensure easy reach
Faridah has some memory problems	
Faridah has difficulty in coordination	
Faridah has some Muslim beliefs	
Faridah is often reluctant to have a wash	
Faridah has some hearing problems	
Faridah has some problematic areas of skin	

Living in a clean and enabling environment

Physical changes in the brain mean that people with dementia are less able to deal with difficulties or risks in the environment. For example, someone may be unable to get around because of poor coordination skills. They may also be less able to take action to minimise the risks of infection e.g. washing their hands after going to the toilet. They may become less motivated and generally less able to think ahead about their health. Poor memory, for example, means that an individual is unable to meet their personal care needs and this would lead to a greater risk of infection in an unclean environment.

A difficult environment can lead to people behaving in ways that are often misunderstood as symptoms of the dementia. The behaviour may actually be symptoms of the environment which can be treated, often fairly simply. If this difference is not recognised it can often mean that the person with dementia is left with additional difficulties that are not a direct result of the dementia.

Problems created by the environment

The following are examples of problems created by the environment rather than by dementia.

- A person with dementia has developed a urinary tract infection in an environment that is not very clean. Staff do not always apply infection control protocols. The person has become more confused. Carers do not notice the urinary tract infection and assume the confusion is part of his dementia. The individual therefore remains unnecessarily disabled.

- A woman with dementia has become incontinent. Staff in the care home put this down to a progression in the dementia. She used to be able to find her way to the toilet but staff have moved some furniture around and often leave wheelchairs blocking access. The woman has therefore been unnecessarily stripped of her dignity as her ability to toilet independently has been removed.

There is a lot we can do to give a person with dementia a better quality of life by changing things in the environment.

This section looks at a range of techniques for communicating with people with dementia.

What you need to learn

- How the behaviour of people with dementia can reflect their feelings and views.
- Developing good listening skills.
- Applying different techniques to support the communication process.

How the behaviour of people with dementia can reflect their feelings and views

The importance of communication

Communication is a two-way process. It is about listening and understanding as well as about expression and talking. It is important to understand the difference between the two because of the different ways that the dementia affects the person who has it. For example, an individual may have difficulty with expression but not understanding, or vice versa, or have difficulties in both areas. Underlying this is the emotional factor that affects a person's ability to want to communicate or to communicate in an appropriate manner.

Expression (talking) →

← Understanding (listening)

Communication is a two-way process

Overcoming difficulties

Communication is important because it is essential for developing positive relationships, to find out what the individual's wishes are, and to offer choices. It also helps you to engage with the person and to encourage them to be as independent as possible. If you use the correct word to prompt an individual it could make the difference between the activity being completed independently or by you. It is your responsibility to ensure that communication is effective with the individual with dementia. This means that *you* must change the way that you communicate in order to meet the person's needs. While you may not always be able to overcome these difficulties, it is essential to try a range of techniques to help in overcoming some of the problems.

Deterioration of language

Different parts of the brain are responsible for different things. In previous sections you have learnt about the deterioration of certain skills, such as the ability to coordinate actions, or the ability to make judgements about spaces. These skills deteriorate because that part of the brain becomes affected by the dementia. The part of the brain that is responsible for language may not be affected immediately but as the condition progresses you might start to see changes in the person's ability to express themselves and to understand.

Think about a person with dementia you work with who has communication difficulties.
How are these difficulties revealed when the person communicates? Can you see any of the common difficulties noted opposite? In what ways have you worked to overcome these?

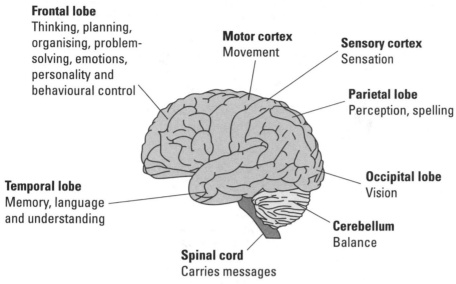

Frontal lobe
Thinking, planning, organising, problem-solving, emotions, personality and behavioural control

Motor cortex
Movement

Sensory cortex
Sensation

Parietal lobe
Perception, spelling

Temporal lobe
Memory, language and understanding

Occipital lobe
Vision

Cerebellum
Balance

Spinal cord
Carries messages

The different parts of the brain and their functions

Problems with expression

People with dementia may encounter different problems in expressing themselves. They may:

- pick incorrect words to express the way they feel
- pick words that are similar in meaning or sound
- use single words to express a feeling
- use garbled or confused words, sometimes known as 'word salad'
- experience problems in concentration
- experience some pain.

Problems with understanding

People with dementia may have the following problems in understanding. They may:

- be unable to understand the context surrounding the communication which gives it meaning
- be unable to recognise certain words
- have difficulty recognising objects, so may not see a toothbrush as a toothbrush
- have difficulty remembering something that is needed to make sense of the sentence
- have a short attention span
- be unable to follow the different parts of the message
- have problems with their hearing or their sight.

Language and feelings

As the disease progresses a person with dementia may completely lose the ability to talk in a rational way, which means that it can be very difficult to understand their spoken words. However, you can always understand someone's feelings and behaviours. It is very important to remember that their perspective on what is happening is often very different to yours. They have lost the ability to make sense of situations because of physical changes to the brain.

A poor memory will also influence the person's understanding of any given situation as previous memories help you to make sense of what is happening in the here and now.

Care scenario: Jean

Jean cannot remember who her carers are from day to day. She also has no insight into her condition and does not recognise that she may need assistance with personal care. Jean is unable to communicate verbally but can clearly express her wishes through her behaviour. One day Jean is sitting in her room when a carer comes in to support her with personal care. The carer tries to talk to Jean but gives up very quickly and then starts to undress her. Jean becomes very angry and starts to shout but the carer dismisses this and continues. Jean then hits the carer.

1. How do you think Jean was feeling when the carer started to undress her?
2. What is Jean's view of the incident?
3. How could the carer have handled the situation better?

Behaviour in communication

It is important that you see the underlying messages in behaviour. If you do not, you run the risk of labelling that individual as a difficult and aggressive person. You should take care when recording incidents because if information is presented in a certain way it can be misunderstood. Examples of this can be found on pages 69–70.

A lot of challenging behaviour comes from the person's difficulty in understanding or communicating. Frustration can then lead to anger. These feelings can be avoided if you take a more informed and understanding approach to meeting an individual's communication needs. Remember that it is *your* responsibility to change the way that you communicate to support the person with dementia.

An individual may behave aggressively for other reasons, such as when they feel insecure, not in control or humiliated. It might be that they find it difficult to process all the information that is being given to them; for example a noisy room may cause real difficulties. You are able to do something about all of these things as they are external factors which involve changes to the environment or changes to the way that you treat someone. However, changes in behaviour can sometimes be caused by internal factors, such as the loss of inhibitions, or changes in a person's judgement skills because of physical changes in the brain.

Think of an incident where a person with dementia has been aggressive.

What was the individual trying to communicate with their behaviour?

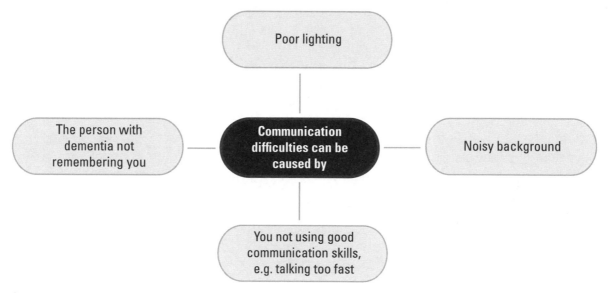

Communication difficulties can be caused by different factors

Kirby LRC
Middlesbrough College
Roman Road
Middlesbrough
TS5 5PJ

Developing good listening skills

Difficulties with communication

Working with someone who has complex communication needs can be difficult. This is because the nature of the condition can affect an individual's communication skills in many different ways, depending on the type and stage of the dementia. It might be difficult for you to understand the person you are working with, or have empathy with the way that they feel.

A person with dementia might see things very differently to you because of the deterioration in the brain; for example an elderly individual might believe that her mother is coming to get her. The way those experiences are communicated to you may be garbled. But the individual often has a desperate need to be understood. By listening and understanding you are able to focus care in the right way.

Your perceptions

If you show the person with dementia that you are actively listening to them you will be demonstrating an act of respect and this is therapeutic in its own right. However, it can be hard to develop good listening skills. For example, your own perceptions of people with dementia may influence the time and patience that you allow to them. Your perceptions about priorities may also influence your ability to take time out to listen to people. You may feel that it is more important to get the individual to the meal table rather than spend the

Sometimes it can be comforting just to have someone listen to you

time listening to their concerns. The consequence of that decision may leave the person feeling vulnerable and uncared for, and could lead to challenging behaviours. A simple action, such as taking the opportunity to listen to someone, can stop you providing inappropriate care and prevent other negative incidents.

Poor listening skills

In order to understand how to listen effectively we must first consider what bad listening is. Often we are unaware of the messages we are giving off when listening to someone. These messages are hidden in our facial expressions and body language. Poor listening can include:

- looking around the room
- not keeping eye contact
- looking at your watch
- sighing
- having your back to someone
- doing something else at the same time
- speaking over someone
- finishing off sentences.

Activity 15

Next time someone is talking to you, try to respond with the bad listening behaviours.

- How long did the conversation last?

_____

- Afterwards, ask the person how they felt.

_____

Good listening skills

Effective listening skills take time and practice. As a bare minimum you should demonstrate in your body language that you respect the person who is talking and have empathy with them.

Effective listening skills will involve:

- a focus on the person
- good eye contact
- nodding and acknowledging that you have heard them
- appropriate facial expressions
- a patient approach, giving the person time to communicate.

You can demonstrate further that you have listened by reflecting back to them what they have said. This should be in a language that they can understand, using simple and short sentences, or non-verbal gestures.

Understanding communication abilities

In order to listen effectively you must have a good understanding of the individual's communication abilities. For example does the person normally communicate using single words? Do they sometimes get words mixed up? Do they have difficulty in finding the correct words?

If you are finding it difficult to understand a person's words look at them and pay attention to:

■ their body language

■ the emotions they are expressing

■ their tone of voice

■ their facial expressions.

It is useful to have a good knowledge of the person's life history, likes and dislikes, as this will also help the process. However, it is important not to make assumptions based on this information.

Different realities

A person with dementia may talk about things from their past, believing that they are happening now. The most important thing of all is that you do not dismiss what the individual is saying as rubbish because of their confusion. This can leave them feeling further confused and humiliated. Instead, acknowledging what a person says is an important way of recognising their emotions. The content of their conversation may not make sense to you but it does to them.

Consider the person with dementia who believes that her mother is alive and frequently asks for her. This need to find mothers is a common reaction for people who feel insecure. If you were to respond to this by contradicting her and stating 'your mother is dead', can you imagine how this would feel? It could be like living the bereavement every day. It would be far more effective to acknowledge the feelings underlying this statement, such as the feeling of insecurity. You could do this by saying, 'I know that you miss your mother and that must be very difficult for you.' By doing this you have reflected back to the individual what she has said, showing that you have listened carefully to her feelings. You have also demonstrated a sense of empathy and trust.

Applying different techniques to support the communication process

Body language – non-verbal communication

If a person with dementia has difficulty understanding what you say they will look for clues in other things to make up for it. For example, an individual may focus on your body language, facial expression or tone of voice. These clues may be interpreted in different ways by people because of different cultural backgrounds. For example, touching may be more appropriate in certain cultures than others.

Touch can often be used in the care of people with dementia to acknowledge their communication or comfort them, particularly where the understanding of verbal communication is limited.

Personal space

Body spacing is important in creating a sense of equality and partnership in a relationship. For example if you stand or sit too close it can feel invasive and overpowering. Standing or sitting too far away can feel uncomforting and indifferent.

Activity 16

While talking with a colleague or family member, adopt the positions shown in the illustrations.

- How do you feel in position one?

_____

- How do you think the person with dementia might feel in position one?

_____

- What is the difference with position two?

_____

Voice tone

Another important factor to consider is tone of voice. We could say the same words with different emotions behind them and the meaning would be experienced differently. People are often unaware of the messages that are given out in their tone of voice.

Activity 17

Try saying the following sentences with the feelings of anger, understanding, impatience and happiness behind them, and hear how differently they sound.

- How are you today?
- What would you like to do today?
- Is there anything I can help you with?

Non-verbal communication

You can use non-verbal communication to engage with a person who has limited verbal skills. However this may not be appropriate in all cases because people's needs vary. Also the dementia may be further complicated by other conditions, such as a stroke, or sensory impairments, such as poor eyesight and hearing. For example, the person may be able to recognise a picture of an object but is unable to recognise the written word. It is important that you use the right technique so that you do not make the individual feel that they have failed in any way.

Activity 18

Below are three case studies. Note in the table which communication techniques would be most suitable for each individual by ticking the relevant box.

Person A

Has a moderate dementia and is blind. However he has good hearing and a good sense of smell. He can understand verbal communication if sentences are simple and short.

Person B

Has advanced dementia and is deaf. She is very responsive to the sense of touch.

Person C

Person C suffered a stroke before developing a dementia. He is unable to understand the written word but can use pictures to communicate how he is feeling.

Technique	Person A	Person B	Person C
Use of body language/gestures			
Facial expressions			
Written words			
Music			
Visuals/pictures			

Activity 18 shows you how varied people's communication needs might be. You should carry out a careful assessment to ensure that you get the correct way of communicating.

Focus on strengths

People with dementia may find it hard to understand complex sentences. Using short, simple sentences can help communication. They also may find it difficult to respond to questions requiring a lot of thought. For example, you might ask

'What would you like to do today?' instead of 'Would you like to go to the park?' The first question requires more complex thought in order to answer. But asking 'closed' questions, which require a yes or no answer, can provide more opportunity for the individual with communication difficulties to respond.

The pace of the sentence should accurately reflect the pace of the listener. People with dementia may find it difficult to understand verbal communication at a normal pace. This is because it might take more time for the brain to process the information; any hearing difficulties will only make the problem worse. You can help by speaking slowly and giving the person plenty of time to listen.

What you can do

There are things that you can do to help communication.

- Find out about the individual's normal method of communication.
- Use short and simple sentences.
- During any conversation focus on the person.
- Make sure that your body language demonstrates that you are listening and that you respect the person.
- Use closed questions.
- Shut out the noise from the rest of the room.
- Do not dismiss what the person is saying as irrelevant or untrue, but instead acknowledge the underlying feelings.
- Try to understand the feelings that drive the behaviour.
- Ensure that the method you use takes account of the person's cultural and religious beliefs.
- Be aware of tone and how this can have a negative effect on the individual.
- Allow enough time for the person to process the information that you have given to them.
- If you do not understand the person, try to get help or look at their body language and consider the emotions underlying this.
- Do not assume that just because someone cannot talk in a logical way they are unable to understand you, or vice versa.
- Do not use abstract phrases in your sentences.

Remember that communication is involved in every aspect of a care plan. Therefore there should be some detail in every part of the care plan about how you engage with the individual, as this may vary in different situations. Make sure that you write down and pass on techniques that work well with the person as it is important to have consistency.

> Make sure that the words you use are non-discriminatory, positive and enabling. There should be a clear focus on a person's strengths during any communication.

In this section you will learn about how a range of therapies can enable a person with dementia to have a better quality of life.

What you need to learn

- Conventional medication.
- Activities.
- Complementary therapies.

Conventional medication

Treating the condition

There is currently no medical cure for dementia. However, medication can slow down the deterioration of the physical changes in the brain. It is important that a diagnosis happens early so that medication can be prescribed, as many types of medication are only effective in certain stages of the condition. Some individuals may miss out on this as they may not report the first symptoms of dementia because of fear. It is also important to find out the type of dementia as some medications will not work with certain dementias.

Doctors may use a test known as the Mini Mental State Examination (MMSE) to determine the stage of a dementia in order to prescribe medication according to national guidelines.

Treating the symptoms

Medication is also used to treat some of the symptoms of dementia. These symptoms may include agitation, hallucinations, anxiety and depression. It is common for people who have dementia to have depression, particularly where they have an insight into their deterioration. Symptoms of depression include loss of weight, reduced appetite, lack of motivation, low mood, increased confusion and poor sleep patterns. However, disrupted sleep could also be a result of poor orientation as to day and night, which is caused by the dementia. Loss of weight and poor nutrition can lead to further difficulties. Some symptoms can mimic those of dementia and therefore may not be treated, or might make diagnosis difficult. Depression can be treated with medication.

Often individuals will also have physical complications related to old age and the treatment of these may be affected by medication that has already been given for the dementia. Therefore changes may be made to normal treatments.

Doctors may be reluctant to prescribe medication that must be taken regularly to someone who may forget to take it. People with dementia in the later stages often require a lot of support and may be living in a residential setting, so are likely to have their medication administered to them. However, a person living in the community, who may wish to remain in control of their medication may on occasions forget to take it. There are assistive technologies and services available to support this, such as a dosset box.

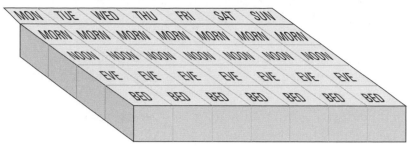

A dosset box can help with the administration of medication

Once someone has been diagnosed with dementia the right to administer their own medication should not be automatically taken away. Carers should consider what can be done to retain independence yet at the same time minimise risks.

Consent and review

It is important to ensure that people consent to the administration of their medication. If an individual disagrees, local policies should be followed.

It is essential to review medication frequently because of the changing nature of both the ageing process and deteriorating conditions such as dementia.

1. What is your organisation's policy about what to do if an individual does not want to take their medication?

2. What are the consequences of not reviewing medication?

Medication and aggression

Medication can be used to treat behavioural disorders such as agitation or aggression. However, a careful approach must be taken as many people with dementia are unnecessarily prescribed medication to manage behaviours and this can cause negative side effects. This may result from a lack of understanding other ways of managing the behaviour or lack of resources.

There are other ways of managing aggressive behaviours that should be explored first, such as the use of activities, complementary therapies or maybe by changing the way the situation is approached.

Over-medication in people who have dementia is a form of abuse.

Hallucinations and sleep disturbance

Medication may be used to treat hallucinations, which are more common in particular kinds of dementia such as a Lewy body dementia. Medication is also used to treat disturbed sleep patterns which are common in people who have dementia.

Sleep problems may occur for a range of reasons, for example the individual may be unaware of the difference between day and night, or may have the two confused. Alternatively, the person may be experiencing some anxiety or agitation during the night. This can lead to mental and physical exhaustion during the day so that the person is unable to function normally. Therefore the use of medication during the night may be beneficial. However, there are side effects to most medications although these can be managed by changing the dose of the medication.

> It is a good idea to try other ways of managing symptoms before turning to medication. A good understanding of the effects of the environment on dementia means you may be more able to change the environment to minimise some symptoms.

Side effects

It is important to have a good understanding of common side effects of the medication used in the treatment of people with dementia. Below are some examples of common side effects.

- Sedation (sleepiness)
- Vomiting and nausea
- Dizziness, unsteadiness
- Stiffness
- Dry mouth
- Constipation
- Headaches.

These side effects could have implications for the individual's care. For example sedation, unsteadiness and dizziness can lead to an increased risk of falls.

Alternatives to medication

Alternatives to medication often work by targeting the root causes of the problems. The table on page 59 shows some examples.

Symptoms caused by dementia	Alternatives to medication
Low mood	May be experienced because of feelings of loss of control and independence. Respecting an individual's rights and developing relationships with them will have a positive effect on mood.
Agitated behaviour	There is good research to indicate that many complementary therapies are effective in reducing incidents of agitation (see page 62).
Aggressive behaviour	Aggressive behaviour may occur because the individual is trying to communicate something to you. If you can identify the message being communicated by observing body language and the underlying emotions, you will be able to prevent those behaviours from repeating.
Sleep problems	If you offer a full and stimulating day programme with a range of appropriate activities, the individual is more likely to sleep well at night.
Wandering	Wandering does not always cause problems. However, if the person goes out of the home and is unsafe, or does not sit down long enough to eat properly, steps may need to be taken. A person may be wandering for different reasons, such as boredom, or because they cannot find their way or are searching for something. Finding meaningful activity during the day will reduce this. Supporting individuals to find their way around might reduce the wandering. If someone is searching for something try to talk to them about the feelings that are underlying this.
Increased confusion caused by poor environment	Confusion can arise from the environment being designed in a way that is not considerate to the person's perceptions and needs. Simple changes to the environment can give the individual increased confidence, less confusion and more independence.
Anxiety	This may occur because the person is frightened of being left alone for long periods of time, worrying that they would be unable to cope. Finding activities to reduce the time that they are alone or more communal living may ease the anxiety.
Psychotic symptoms	Individuals may see or hear things that are not real. Some hallucinations can be frightening in nature and generally upsetting, and therefore should be treated. However, not all hallucinations are negative, for example, the person who sets additional places at the table for her imagined friends who keep her company. Not all hallucinations need to be treated, however sometimes they can lead to behaviours which cause harm. A careful assessment will need to be completed. Hallucinations are less likely to occur when the individual is kept busy with an activity.

Activities

Some activities can effectively prevent difficult behaviours. They are also important in maintaining the individual's sense of purpose and self-esteem. Activities can provide stimulation by enabling the person with dementia to remain more alert. Joint activities are an enjoyable way of building and maintaining relationships and generally providing much-needed social stimulation.

However, many activities are delivered without any thought about some of the impairments and difficulties the individual faces as a result of the dementia. Activities which are not designed to meet the specific needs of the individual can leave that person feeling excluded and humiliated. For example a quiz is not appropriate for a person that is unable to think on that level or read written words.

A film is not appropriate if an individual's memory is so poor that they cannot follow the story line.

A combination of factors may result in someone being unable to take part in an activity at all. For example, if an individual has poor coordination skills, poor judgement and is unable to move their limbs freely, they will be unable to play even seated ball games.

> Any activity must seek to maximise the strengths and remaining skills of the person with dementia.

Types of activity

There are many different types of activity that can be used to help people with dementia. Some are outlined below. You can get further advice and information from skilled and qualified therapists.

Reminiscence

Reminiscence is often used to stimulate memory. Individuals may be able to recognise pictures and may have their long-term memory intact. Therefore this activity focuses on these strengths.

Life story work

A range of materials could be used in this activity to engage the individual at the appropriate level. This activity has its own therapeutic worth and also enables you to build up a good picture of the person's life, which can enrich relationships and help with their care.

Art activities

Different art activities can be used as an occupational activity but also as a form of communication.

Daily activities

Even the most mundane activities, such as setting the table or helping to clear away, can provide the person with dementia with a sense of purpose and self-esteem.

Sensory stimulation

This activity is often used when individuals have a progressed dementia but their sense of smell and touch is still intact. There is more information about this on page 63.

Activity 19

When planning an activity you need to consider all of the factors below. Use the table to carry out an assessment of a person with dementia who you know.

Internal factors	External factors
Concentration span	Is the environment arranged in a way that does not increase confusion?
Extent of memory problems	Do the people in the group work well together?
Ability to follow a sequence	Will the range of noises in the environment increase confusion?
Ability to initiate thought and action	Has the care worker got the necessary communication skills to engage with the person?
Medication (activities may be more effective at different times of the day)	
Communication needs	
Physical abilities (for example the freedom with which they can move parts of their body)	
Ability to judge spaces (for example when throwing a ball)	
Past hobbies and interests	

Complementary therapies

Complementary therapies cover a diverse range of theories and philosophies. Therapies thought to be useful for dementia are:

- herbal medicine
- acupuncture
- aromatherapy and massage
- sensory therapy
- music therapy.

These therapies can be used alongside conventional medicine to improve the symptoms of dementia and the individual's quality of life.

Herbal medicine

Herbal medicine involves the use of plants to restore or maintain health. The quality of herbal products available from shops varies greatly and it is important to buy recognised brands from a leading manufacturer. Herbal medicines can be taken as tablets, capsules or as liquid extract.

The most well-researched herbal product in the west for dementia is gingko biloba. In clinical trials it has been found to improve quality of life for both the individual and their carers. It has recently been recommended for the health services. It is also thought to be able to slow down the progression of dementia. Herbalists believe this is because gingko greatly improves blood flow to the brain.

The most important factor to consider in the use of herbal medicines is interaction with other medications. Gingko biloba is a herbal blood-thinning drug therefore certain conventional medications should not be given with this (see table below).

Medication	Potential effect if mixed with gingko
Warfarin, heparin and any other anticoagulants	Over-thinning of the blood causing haemorrhaging and stroke

Lemon balm, also known as melissa, is thought to help prevent the loss of a brain chemical called acetylcholine. Lemon balm makes a pleasant tea.

Acupuncture

Acupuncture originated in China but is now widespread in the west. The treatment uses very fine needles to unblock energy pathways to help restore health. It is thought to be useful for dementia by helping the symptoms and perhaps slowing down mental decline. Acupuncture is not suitable for people who have a fear of needles.

Aromatherapy and massage

Both aromatherapy and massage have been found to be useful for people with dementia and many individuals can benefit from these therapies.

Lavender oil has been found to be particularly effective in reducing agitation and emotional symptoms. Lemon balm is an aromatherapy oil that may help the decline in mental abilities because it can prevent the loss of the brain chemical acetylcholine.

Massage has also been found to improve a person's emotional symptoms. Even simple hand massages combined with lavender oil have been shown to be beneficial. However, on occasion, it can cause agitation in some people and it is important to be able to recognise this when it happens.

Some individuals suffer from a reduced sense of smell as a part of their dementia. These people will benefit more from massage alone.

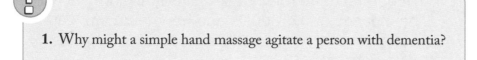

1. Why might a simple hand massage agitate a person with dementia?

Sensory therapy

Sensory therapy aims to stimulate the senses of sight, hearing and touch in order to improve mood, decrease agitation and promote communication. Sensory rooms providing projections of abstract images, bubble tubes with mirrors and coloured lighting, mirror balls, musical backgrounds and soft balls and spike rings have been shown to be useful for all of the symptoms mentioned above.

Activity 20

Can you think how to provide basic sensory therapy activities for the individual in a day-to-day care-giving environment?

Sense	Activity
Sight	
Sound	
Touch	

Music therapy

Music therapy has been shown to help improve memory, health and identity in people with dementia. Often, long-term memory is still good so individuals continue to be able to sing old songs. Even after language deteriorates, musical abilities appear to be preserved. People with dementia may still be able to play pieces of music previously learned, despite no longer being able to identify the composer or song.

Music and song is thought to be able to give the person a sense of accomplishment, to energise and stimulate, and to trigger words. It can soothe and comfort both the person with dementia and their care giver. Music may also relieve some of the behavioural and emotional consequences of dementia – especially in the later stages.

Carers can help provide a very basic form of music therapy activity by simply humming or singing. This may encourage the individual to do the same.

You might face the following difficulties when helping a person to join in with a music activity:

- shyness, lack of confidence in both person with dementia and care giver.
- difficulty choosing music/songs that have significance and meaning for the individual.

The important thing to remember is that it is not what the individual sounds like, but the enjoyment they may gain from the activity.

2 Roles, responsibilities and boundaries

2.1 Understand the roles, responsibilities and boundaries of individuals and how team work and support can lead to better support of individuals with dementia

What you need to learn

In this section you are going to learn about the role and nature of support services in providing better care to the person with dementia. It will cover:

- individual
- family and friends of the individual
- independent advocate
- care worker

- manager
- social worker
- GP
- specialist personnel.

Are the people with dementia who you work with aware of their care plan? If not, why not?

Do you involve the individual in the decisions about their care? If not, why not?

Individual

The person with dementia needs to participate as much as possible so that you can provide the most effective care. They have to be central to the decisions about their care and encouraged to be as independent as possible. An individual's views should be regularly documented as their views form an important part of the decision-making process. Rather than providing services *to* an individual, care should be carried out *with* an individual. If this is not happening in your organisation or in your practice you have a personal responsibility to question why. This may involve some reflection on your own assumptions, values and beliefs about people with dementia.

Family and friends of the individual

Family and friends provide an invaluable source of care to the person with dementia. This might be direct care, supervision or low level monitoring, doing the shopping or managing finances. Often in the early to middle stages of the condition, family are likely to provide a substantial amount of care to the person with dementia and may themselves frequently require support from a range of services.

Independent advocate

Changes in legislation have meant that independent advocates are now playing a bigger role in the care of people with dementia. It is also increasingly realised that the views of people with dementia are often not heard but are important. Independent advocates often have good knowledge of the issues that affect people with dementia as well as appropriate communication skills. Independent advocates might be involved in representing the individual's wishes at meetings with other professionals about future care needs, financial matters and wishes relating to any aspect of the individual's current care.

Care worker

Care workers often work with an individual to meet their day-to-day needs. They will be involved in observing and reporting on any changes in the person's condition and providing practical and emotional support. Next to family members, care workers have the greatest opportunity to affect the quality of life for the person with dementia. This can be achieved by understanding the condition, focusing on strengths and encouraging maximum participation from the individual in order to retain their skills. The role of the care worker is important because they often have to implement a large part of the care plan. It is therefore essential that they also understand the limitations of their role and understand those of other support services which complement their care.

Care workers can work across a range of services such as home care, hospitals, clinics, day care, residential or nursing care. The basic elements of their role will not vary too much between these settings but their responsibilities might. For example, they will not be responsible for administering medications in some of these settings.

Carers may attend a range of meetings to report on their observations, or to represent the individual's views. Senior carers will be responsible for the coordination of care plans. Carers require extensive on the job training, including a minimum NVQ level 2 in Care.

Manager

A manager may be responsible for managing a range of dementia-related services. These could be residential homes, home care, nursing care or day care, or a specific outreach service. Their main role is to ensure that standards are maintained within the care service; for example to ensure that an adequate assessment of the individual's needs has been completed and is monitored regularly.

A manager will often have extensive experience in that care setting, or a professional qualification such as social work, nursing or NVQ level 4 in Care. They have a role in alerting a social worker if they feel that the individual's care needs are not being met. They will liaise with a range of primary care services, such as opticians, chiropodists and general practitioners, to get advice and arrange for interventions to take place. They will also liaise with family members within any setting to gather information for their assessment and to obtain their views about the care.

Social worker

A social worker will receive a referral requesting an assessment for support services for either the individual or their informal carer. This request may come from a professional, the individual, a member of the family, a neighbour or friend. The local authority, which employs social workers, is legally bound to carry out an assessment of need to identify the appropriate support services. Criteria are applied to identify whether the individual is entitled to those services. If so, a further financial assessment may be applied to determine whether the individual should pay towards the cost of the care.

The social worker will work with a range of people to get the information that they need to complete the assessment. This would certainly include the individual and GP but may also involve psychiatric services such as a community psychiatric nurse (CPN) as well as some specialist personnel (see below). The social worker may also seek additional information and guidance from voluntary organisations which have specialist areas of information and may need to involve an advocate in the assessment stage.

Once the assessment is completed, the social worker will put together a package of care. This will involve liaising with a range of service providers, such as home care, residential or day care and so on. The social worker will then monitor and review the package of care to ensure that it is continually meeting the individual's needs.

General Practitioner (GP)

The GP is often the first person that the individual comes in contact with. The GP may make a preliminary diagnosis but it is likely that they will refer an individual to a psycho-geriatrician or specialist in dementia care to make a diagnosis or carry out more extensive investigations. The GP is often the main referral route for all other primary care services in the community and therefore typically liaises with a range of professionals. A GP will work with nurses in addressing concerns and supporting the review of medication.

Specialist personnel

There is a range of specialist personnel that make up the team of people involved in the assessment and care of someone with dementia. These people include the following:

Occupational therapist (OT)

The OT is responsible for assessing the person's ability to carry out a range of activities of daily living, such as having a bath. From this assessment they will provide aids and adaptations to enable the person to be more independent. Occupational therapists work in specific areas such as stroke, rehab, mental health etc. Occupational therapists who work with people with dementia have an in-depth knowledge of how the condition affects the ability to carry out daily care and can recommend techniques to overcome some of these barriers.

Physiotherapist

Physiotherapists are responsible for enabling a person with dementia to regain some functional ability, such as walking, and often they will carry out assessments for walking aids. A physiotherapist will also be able to give some guidance on the risk of falls and guidance on safe methods of transferring an individual. Physiotherapists often work very closely with occupational therapists.

Speech and language therapist

Speech and language therapists are responsible for supporting people to regain speech. They can also give detailed guidance on communication techniques to use. Speech and language therapists are involved in assessment of swallowing capabilities and will normally work very closely with a dietician.

Psychologist

A psychologist is involved in some of the testing of the brain function in diagnosing the dementia. They also provide behavioural therapy if required.

Psychiatric nurse

Psychiatric nurses are also involved in some of the assessment of the brain function and may carry out some similar assessment processes as the psychologist. They work in acute settings and in the community and are responsible for monitoring medical interventions.

Registered General Nurse

Nurses are involved in the assessment and treatment of physical conditions affecting the person with dementia. Many of the conditions may be related to old age. They may work in hospitals or in the community.

Psychiatrist

A psychiatrist who specialises in dementia care is known as a psycho-geriatrician. They are involved in the diagnosis and treatment of people with dementia. They often coordinate a team of some of the other professionals from a range of disciplines.

Dietician

Dieticians are responsible for assessing a person's nutritional needs. They will work closely with other professionals to ensure that the individual maintains good physical health.

Multi-disciplinary teams

The factors affecting people with dementia can be social, physical or mental, and are often complex. Many professionals work in multi-disciplinary teams to enable them to understand the interplay of issues better. Each professional may carry out an assessment and input this at a multi-disciplinary meeting where all the issues are discussed together in order to come up with a holistic assessment of need.

Activity 21

Write the name of the professional who you think would best meet an individual's needs in the table below. Sometimes there may be an overlap of roles.

Need	Professional
An individual is finding it difficult to get into the bath	
An individual has recently had difficulty eating and lost a lot of weight	
An individual has lost some muscle strength in their legs after a stay in hospital	
An individual is displaying dementia-like symptoms	
An individual has an ulcer on the leg that needs to be dressed	
An individual has been prescribed some anti-depressants that need to be monitored	

In this section you will learn about contributing positively to your organisation's recording processes in a way that adds value to the care of people with dementia.

What you need to learn

- Distinguishing between fact and opinion in recordings.
- Different types of recordings in the care environment.
- Consequences of using inappropriate and negative language.

Distinguishing between fact and opinion in recordings

Recordings are an important part of your work. You need to write things down so that you can:

- inform your colleagues about what has happened
- provide care in a consistent way
- monitor how effective the care is
- record the wishes of a person with dementia
- understand the individual's needs better
- record any changes to the individual's needs
- use the information to inform a review of the care by looking back at what has happened
- understand recurrent themes that may highlight problems or concerns
- understand what the dangers are through documenting risk assessments
- check accountability.

Recording and reviewing

Dementia is a condition that may change rapidly. The individual may also be elderly, which means that there are often other physical changes taking place in addition to the dementia. For these reasons it is important to constantly review and understand the needs of a person with dementia. This involves recording what you have observed and the action that you have taken, communicating with your colleagues and reading what other people have written.

The consequences of not taking this seriously could be poor practice or even death. For example, if the individual's wishes and beliefs are not recorded, care could be provided in a way that is not in accordance with their wishes – often leaving the individual feeling not respected and demoralised. A more serious consequence – if changes in physical health are not clearly documented or administration of medication not clearly recorded – is that the individual could die.

Activity 22

In the table below write down the consequences of not doing the things listed.

What you should do	Consequences of not doing
Communicate to your colleagues what has happened	
Provide care in a consistent way	
Monitor the care that you deliver	
Record the individual's wishes	
Record any changes to the individual's needs	
Use information to inform a review of the care by looking back at what has happened	
Understand recurrent themes that may highlight problems or concerns	
Understand the individual's needs better	
Understand what the dangers are through documenting risk assessments	
Demonstrate the work that you have carried out	

When you have to communicate something important to one of your colleagues about an individual's care, this should be done in a confidential way and should be written down.

Fact and opinion

The quality of the recording is very important. One of the factors determining quality is whether or not the recording is written objectively and is fact-based.

Writing objectively is when you separate your personal beliefs from what you are writing about – it is fact-based. Writing subjectively is when you allow your personal beliefs to influence what you have written – it is opinion-based. However, it is often easier to write subjectively as you might find it difficult to detach how you feel from what you are writing.

In the first section of this book you learnt about how your perceptions, values and belief systems can influence your behaviour towards a person with dementia. Recordings that are written subjectively can influence the thoughts and perceptions of the reader. This is shown in Activity 23 on page 70.

Activity 23

Can you tell which of the statements below are fact-based and which are opinion-based?

Statement	Fact-based ✓ or X	Opinion-based ✓ or X
1. I feel that Maria was very upset today and will probably become quite disruptive later.		
2. I saw Maria crying this morning after she came out of the bath.		
3. The room had boxes piled high and there was newspaper scattered on the floor.		
4. The room was very messy and John had clearly not been coping.		
5. Marsha has been stealing things from everybody's rooms; she is a thief and a liar.		
6. Marsha had a brush in her room which belonged to another resident.		

Some of the statements in Activity 23 may need further investigation. It is important not to make assumptions but instead to find out the facts.

Points to consider

Before completing a recording consider the following.

- What are the facts?
- Are they relevant for this particular record?
- Have I involved the individual as much as possible in the recording?
- What structure should I use?
- Is the input from other people clearly referenced?
- Is it written in respectful language?
- Have I written about strengths as well as negatives?

Poor recordings

Poor recordings are common in care work. This may be because care workers do not realise they should be making reports in a written form. It may also be because there is a perception that recordings are only required to highlight problems and difficulties. However, when caring for a person with a condition that is progressive it is essential to recognise and acknowledge their strengths. A focus on these will ensure that care is provided in a way that involves the individual, creating much greater self-esteem. Writing about strengths should be an integral part of all assessments, care planning and daily recordings for people with dementia.

Another reason for poor recordings may be because of the difficulty in identifying the individual's expressed wishes and needs or response to care. A process called 'dementia care mapping' is a detailed approach to observation and recordings that highlight the quality of care. It helps in developing ways of improving this. There are many organisations offering training on dementia care mapping.

Activity 22 on page 69 showed the consequences of not putting in place proper systems of recordings. The illustration below highlights some other common problems with recordings.

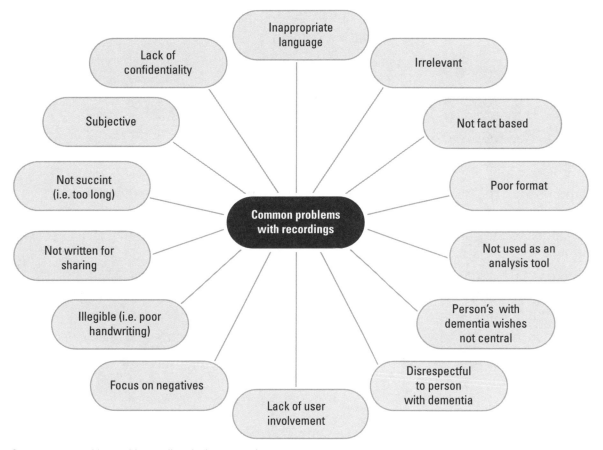

Some common problems with recordings in the care environment

Different types of recordings in the care environment

Different recordings have different purposes. It is important that you fully understand the purpose of the record before reading it and then recording in it yourself.

Information on different types of records follows. Not all organisations will use all these records, or they may use them in a slightly different way, so it is important to understand the purpose of the records within your organisation. The person you care for could suffer if records are not used correctly.

Diary

The diary usually sets out general activities that are taking place. This might include new admissions and out-patient appointments. However, care should be taken not to write down the names of individuals as this record is often not kept as securely as personal files.

Accident book

This is used to document accidents that have taken place. This information will be referred to later to learn more about preventing accidents.

Visitor's sign-in book

The purpose of a sign-in visitor's book is to determine:

- who is in the building – records name, time in and out
- where they are likely to be – records person visiting.

Daily log

The purpose of the daily log is to monitor changes to the care plan (deterioration and improvement), any expressed wishes, and action taken.

- Changes to the care plan – deterioration or improvement of mental, physical and social needs.
- Expressed wishes – how did the individual respond to care being given? This could be recorded under behaviour but ensure that this is recorded factually and that no assumptions are made.
- Action taken – what actions did you carry out? Which were effective and which were not?
- Difficulties in the delivery of care – this might include health and safety concerns for example.

Care plan

The purpose of this record is to set out how the care will be carried out; for example what support needs an individual has and how these can best be met. Care plans are documents that are usually updated following a review.

Handover book

This record is used to hand over specific tasks that still need to be completed. This record will form the basis of the handover meeting. As with the diary, this record will often not detail specific names for reasons of confidentiality.

Medication Administration Record (MAR) chart

This chart identifies what medication an individual is taking and how and when this is administered. This chart is completed by trained staff only and states when medication is administered or refused.

Pressure sore risk assessment

This will normally be completed by trained personnel. It will show an assessment of an individual's skin and identify what has been done to minimise the risks. This is reviewed and updated periodically, or when changes happen.

Safer moving and handling risk assessment

As with the pressure sore risk assessment, this will normally be completed by trained staff. It will set out all of the factors that influence the way that you would manoeuvre a patient and set out what can be done to minimise any risks. This is reviewed and updated periodically, or when changes happen.

Reports

Reports are required for a variety of reasons but you will usually need to state what the purpose is. The beginning will describe the way the information was gathered (method for the research), the middle should provide details of the findings and the conclusion will offer some recommendations. Remember that this must be an objective representation of the events.

Activity 24

In the table below, note down the purpose of each record and what might happen if the record is not read and used by carers.

Type of record	Purpose	Consequences if not read
Diary		
Accident book		
Visitor's sign-in book		
Daily log		
Care plan		
Handover book		
Medication Administration Record (MAR) chart		
Pressure sore risk assessment		
Safer moving and handling risk assessment		

Consequences of using inappropriate and negative language

The language that is used in recordings can sometimes be hurtful and disrespectful. The Data Protection Act states that everyone has access to their own records, so when completing a record you should always have in your mind, 'Is this record written for sharing?' It is essential to write in a way that upholds the individual's rights and treats the person with dignity and respect.

When reporting issues, you have a personal responsibility to ensure that it is done in a manner which is respectful to the client. In addition to this, you should challenge any reports you read that are not respectful to the individual.

Activity 25

Below are two extracts from daily recordings that have been written about the same individual but by different people.

Extract 1

Mary sat in her room today and listened to her television but despite this was a difficulty. She had the television on loudly and would often shout in response to it. Every time someone walked past the room Mary became very agitated and would scream in a high-pitched voice. At lunchtime Mary was very naughty as she refused to eat much of her food, and kept banging her cup on the table. Her noise could be heard from down the corridor. I tried to talk to Mary but she was mad. All of the words were crazy and she was just talking rubbish.

Extract 2

Mary sat in her room today and kept stating, 'Not feeling well'. Despite this Mary watched an old film that was on the television which stimulated her, as she was laughing loudly at points. Mary often tried to alert other people to the film as they walked past the room. Mary was able to clearly express her wishes regarding her lunch; she ate very little. I reported to the nurse in charge that Mary had been stating repeatedly 'Not feeling well' and that she had not eaten much of her lunch.

- Would you *perceive* Mary differently if you had only read extract 1?

  _____

  _____

- Do you think that you might *treat* Mary differently if you had only read extract 1?

  _____

  _____

- Circle the negative words that are written in extract 1.

- What strengths have been highlighted in extract 2?

  _____

  _____

The way that your reports are represented could influence the way that the reader perceives the individual and consequently behaves towards them.

This section covers the different types of care provision available to support people with dementia. There are many different support services available, both for people with dementia and their families. The range of services reflects the different needs and personal choices of the individuals. Many people with dementia will use a number of different services as their needs increase.

What you need to learn

- Domiciliary, respite care and day services.
- Hospitals.
- Care homes with personal care or nursing care.
- Sheltered accommodation and supported housing.
- Voluntary and charitable organisations.

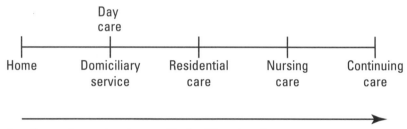

A continuum of support services provides for different needs

Domiciliary, respite care and day services

This range of services supports those who live in the community. Services are provided not only by local authorities but also by private and voluntary sector organisations. Domiciliary care is care in the home and will often involve support with personal care and domestic tasks such as shopping. These services are designed to enable people to remain in their own homes for as long as possible and to make this as safe as possible.

Access to domiciliary care is usually through the social services department, which carries out a Community Care Assessment. This identifies which level of service is required, which services will be provided and if assistive technologies or aids are required. This is known as care management. Home visits can be short, sometimes only lasting fifteen minutes at a time, and may focus on a specific task. This service might be supplemented with informal care such as that provided by a close relative or friend. Home care may also be supplemented by day care, where an individual is able to receive social stimulation and be supervised in a safe environment.

Respite care can be provided for short breaks, of perhaps one to two weeks, to give the informal carers a break from caring.

A Community Care Assessment will indicate whether someone is at risk if being left at home for long periods unsupervised. An individual will always have a choice about the level of service that they receive and cannot be forced to accept a service if they are able to make informed choices. Many people initially find it difficult to accept that they need support from different services, particularly when this involves allowing a stranger into their home.

A good home care service for people with dementia needs to have a high level of consistency; for example, home care services which tend to rotate carers a lot can cause much confusion for someone who has memory problems.

Many home care services that do not allow enough time to work in a way that encourages independence are likely to create dependency. Home care services which do not consider the specific needs of people with dementia lead to more hospital admissions that could actually be avoided.

Hospitals

Most people with dementia are admitted to hospital when they become physically unwell. Sometimes they are admitted suddenly through an accident and emergency department because they are at risk of immediate harm. Hospitals are very confusing places for people with dementia. They can make them appear more confused than they really are, which can lead to too many people being admitted to care homes from hospital.

Care homes

There are two levels of care homes – residential and nursing. Residential care is for people who need to be supervised, or who need more support than can be given in the community. People in residential settings have more independence than those in nursing settings. People in nursing homes usually need care provided by trained nurses and are often more dependent. Special training is required to work with people with dementia. If a person has had a formal diagnosis of dementia, they will not be accepted into a care home that is not registered as such.

Sheltered accommodation and supported housing

Sheltered accommodation consists of a number of homes or flats together in one unit. There is a warden on site, but the warden does not carry out personal care and there is no overnight supervision. Home carers can provide personal care in sheltered accommodation. There is also a type of supported housing which is often referred to as extra care sheltered housing. This level of service could be seen as being between care in the home and residential care. It offers people with dementia a real opportunity to live in a safer environment with privacy.

Voluntary and charitable organisations

Voluntary and charitable organisations have a key role in educating and supporting other services. Organisations such as the Alzheimer's Society provide information and advice in the form of factsheets and a website. They also have nationwide carers groups which support informal carers. Age Concern support day centres and 'meals on wheels', and also provide a range of advice and information sheets.

Defining dementia

3.1 Understand the definition of dementia and the
difference between dementia, depression and
confusional states. Understand the importance
of diagnosis and the implications for support and
the care of the individual

In this section you are going to learn about the importance of recognising other conditions
that have similar symptoms to dementia so that individuals can gain access to the
appropriate treatment.

Definitions

There are important differences between dementia, confusional states and depression.

Condition	Definition
Dementia	An irreversible brain disorder affecting different parts of the brain, causing an effect on a range of functions.
Confusional states	Sometimes known as 'delirium', this is a reversible state that is a direct consequence of a physical illness or is a result of intoxication.
Depression	This is a disorder creating feelings of sadness and hopelessness.

Confusional states and depression are both common in people with dementia. You might
find it difficult to tell the difference between symptoms caused by the dementia and
symptoms caused by confusional states and depression. This is because the symptoms
are very similar. However, the treatments for some are more effective than for others. This
means that by identifying the correct causes, working together with the medical staff, it is
likely that many of these symptoms can be treated. The danger of not recognising depression or a confusional state is that you might not treat them but instead put their symptoms down to the dementia.

Symptoms and causes of depression

Common symptoms experienced by someone with depression includes:

- lack of motivation
- excessive sadness
- not sleeping well at night
- lack of appetite
- memory problems
- difficulty concentrating.

Depression can be caused by:

- something internal (endogenous)
- a reaction to an incident (reactive) such as a bereavement, admission to residential care, knowing that there has been a diagnosis of dementia, loss of independence, or periods of isolation and loneliness.

Symptoms and causes of confusional states

Common symptoms experienced by someone who has a confusional state includes:

- poor concentration
- fluctuating consciousness
- language disturbance
- disorientation
- seeing things differently (perceptual difficulties).

Some of the causes of confusional states include:

- infections
- thyroid dysfunction
- dehydration
- intoxication through drugs
- respiratory problems.

1. Which symptoms found in dementia are also found in depression and confusional states?

If you are concerned about a person with dementia you should refer them to the GP. The GP might want to find out the following.

- Has there been a major life event recently?
- How long have the symptoms persisted?
- Was there a rapid onset?
- What changes have there been to the physical state of the individual?
- What drugs (prescribed and non-prescribed) has the individual taken?
- Is there a pattern to the confusion – has it fluctuated?

The GP may carry out further biological screening, such as blood or urine tests, to determine the cause of the symptoms.

Treating these conditions can make a very big difference to the quality of someone's life. It may mean an individual can:

- do more for themselves
- live in their own home
- feel happier in their lives.

It is important to understand the difference between dementia, depression and confusional states because the treatments are not the same for all three.

Depression can be treated with a range of therapies, such as antidepressants, structured activities or just by talking to someone. Confusional states can be treated by treating the underlying physical cause.

Why diagnosis is important

The process of diagnosis can be an emotionally painful and humiliating experience for people with dementia and their families. However, once a diagnosis has been made, the individual is able to access a range of support services to help them. Informal carers will be able to access information on how to support their loved one and themselves during the progression of the dementia.

A person may first contact their GP who can carry out some preliminary tests, but the GP may also refer the individual to a specialist doctor. It can be difficult to get an accurate picture of the type of dementia and this can only truly be determined after the person has died, at a post-mortem.

The specialist may make a decision based on a range of information, including:

- mental tests, sometimes known as a mini mental state test, designed to test a range of brain functions
- a history of the decline and information about the range of symptoms
- consideration of physical factors, which may require a brain scan
- questions about how the person is coping with their daily living.

There are different types of dementia and the specialist may be able to diagnose the type based on the information gathered during the assessment.

It is important to learn about the types of dementia for four main reasons:

1. You can plan care better by:
   - understanding common symptoms and providing care in a way to support these
   - telling the difference between what is caused by the dementia and what is caused by other factors
   - understanding strengths and making the most of them. For example, because the different types of dementia affect the brain in different ways, some strengths may remain for longer in certain types of dementia.

2. You can relate better by:
   - having empathy with the individual because you understand how the particular dementia affects them
   - understanding how communication is affected by that particular kind of dementia.

3. The individual can plan their future better by:
   - understanding their care needs better
   - making arrangements about their affairs
   - having time to talk to their families.

4. The individual may be able to receive more accurate medical support.

- Some medical treatments only work on some kinds of dementia.
- Some treatments for symptoms may make certain dementias worse.

Activity 26 relates to sections 3.1 and 3.2. It will encourage you to think about *why* diagnosis is important, i.e. the implications for care. Diagnosis is not just about dementia but the type of dementia.

Every person with dementia is unique. It is important not to make assumptions about a person's needs based on their diagnosis alone.

Activity 26

Read the definitions of the different types of dementia given on pages 83–85. In the table below write down what implications each will have for the care that is received.

Type of dementia	Implications for care
Alzheimer's disease	
Vascular dementia	
Pick's disease	
Dementia with Lewy bodies	
Creutzfeld Jakob Disease (CJD)	
Huntington's disease	

3.2. Understand the most common types and causes of dementia

In this section you are going to learn about some of the most common types of dementia and their symptoms.

Dementia is the term that is used to describe the symptoms of a condition. There are more than 100 different types of dementia and in this section you are going to learn about the most common ones.

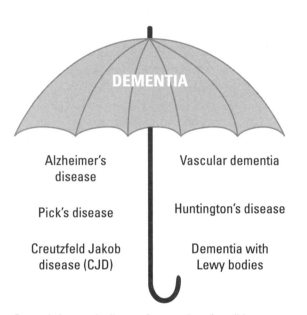

Alzheimer's disease

Vascular dementia

Pick's disease

Huntington's disease

Creutzfeld Jakob disease (CJD)

Dementia with Lewy bodies

Dementia is an umbrella term for a number of conditions

It is important to understand the diagnosis, but it is also important that you see the person first, before seeing the diagnosis.

It can be very difficult to try to understand the physiological changes in the brain. You do not need to know this in a lot of detail, as it is more important to understand that there are different types and that there are benefits for you and the individual to understand what these are. Some basic details about the types of dementia and how these present themselves are shown on the next few pages. You can find out more from the Alzheimer's Society by visiting their website which you can access by going to www. heinemann.co.uk/hotlinks and entering the express code 2307P.

Discussing a diagnosis with a person can be difficult as 'dementia' can be a frightening word. You should choose your language carefully and be aware of the impact the diagnosis has on the individual and their family.

Alzheimer's disease

Alzheimer's disease is a progressive condition where brain cells die. There are about three-quarters of a million people in the UK with some form of dementia and Alzheimer's is the most common form (55 per cent of cases). This condition typically has a longer term than many of the other dementias, and may last up to 20 years. The direct cause of the condition is unknown but a small proportion of cases can be hereditary.

The first signs of the condition are usually memory loss and mood swings. These changes progress gradually as more of the brain cells die, leading to increased loss of function in other areas. The deterioration pattern of this condition is usually a gradual one and can affect all areas of the brain. An individual at the beginning, middle and end stages of the disease will need very different care.

People with Down's Syndrome are at an increased risk of developing Alzheimer's disease. Support and guidance for this condition should be sought from an agency dealing specifically with this issue.

Vascular dementia

This is the second most common form of dementia; about 20 per cent of people with dementia have this type. Vascular dementia is caused by a decrease in the blood supply to the brain, which causes brain cells to die. A number of factors can influence the blood supply to the brain, including heart problems, diabetes and high blood pressure.

The deterioration pattern is different to that in Alzheimer's as it is typically in a step-wise fashion. This is because the deterioration is triggered by an event such as a small stroke, therefore the individual may stay at the same level of ability for some time before there is another change. When there are many small strokes to the brain this is known as a multi-infarct dementia. Many people with this form of dementia are likely to have depression as well. An individual may also be experiencing some physical problems related to a stroke, such as a one-sided weakness.

Vascular dementia is irreversible, however some medication can minimise the risks of multiple strokes. A healthier lifestyle may also reduce the risk. This condition can exist with other types of dementia; for example, an individual may have Alzheimer's disease and vascular dementia as well.

How would you feel if you were diagnosed with a form of dementia?

What action would you take after this?

How important would it be to you to have the right information?

Although it is important to understand the stages of dementia, you must also remember that everyone is different and will deteriorate at different rates.

Pick's disease

This condition affects about 5 per cent of people with dementia. It is a degenerative disease that starts by affecting the frontal and temporal lobes of the brain. Early symptoms include problems with behaviour and language. People affected by this condition may become uninhibited, not caring about what others may think, for example, they may take their clothes off in public or become more extrovert in their behaviour.

Other functions of the brain may remain in the early stages, such as understanding where they are and what time of day it is (this is known as orientation) and memory. Therefore initial diagnosis may be difficult as there are no obvious memory problems or confusion. The pattern of the progression of the disease can vary. In the later stages of the condition other functions of the brain are affected, but typically the damage to the brain is in one area.

Dementia with Lewy bodies

About 15 per cent of people with dementia have this condition. Lewy bodies are bits of protein that are found in the nerve cells. As they develop they interrupt the proper functioning of the brain. Common symptoms include hallucinations, stiffness, shakes and problems with walking (similar to Parkinson's disease). They can also have difficulties judging spaces and can be at a higher risk of falls.

There is no specific treatment for this condition and some medication has a negative effect on the condition, so early and correct diagnosis is important.

Creutzfeld Jakob Disease (CJD)

Sometimes known as CJD, this is a degenerative condition causing brain cells to die. It will often have a rapid onset and decline: most cases last about one year from diagnosis to death. Younger people can be affected by this condition. A CJD brain will have very tiny holes in it where the damage has occurred.

CJD can be caused in different ways as it can be inherited or transmitted. It was first diagnosed in the UK in 1996 as the variant form of CJD, found in infected beef. Some people may carry the virus for up to 30 years before they are affected by it.

Initial signs of the condition are memory difficulties or mood swings. As the disease progresses other areas of the brain are affected. This can cause stiffness, jerking movements and difficulties with mobility.

Huntington's disease

Huntington's disease is a hereditary condition that often affects people at a much younger age, between 30 and 50 years. If the condition develops before the age of 20 it is known as juvenile HD. This condition is degenerative and affects a specific part of the brain called the basal ganglia. The condition affects about one in every 10,000 people.

In the early stages, symptoms include involuntary movements, memory loss and changing emotions such as aggressive outbursts or depression. The condition also affects the individual's ability to organise and plan.

People with dementia may be affected in different ways, as the way the brain alters differs in each condition. But every person with dementia is still able to experience and express a range of emotions. You need to consider this with every encounter with the individual who has dementia.

Activity 27

The different types of dementia vary in important ways. In the table below write why this information might be important. The first box has been completed to help you.

Differences in types of dementia	Reason why difference is important
Types of early symptoms	Help diagnosis
Young age at onset	
Older age at onset	
Gradual pattern of decline	
Step-wise pattern of decline	
Skills maintained	
Common physical conditions related to the type of dementia	
Hereditary condition	
Symptom change over the course of the condition	
Insight into changes	

In this section you will learn about some common signs and symptoms of dementia. It is important to understand these as it will help you to provide care in a way that supports people's strengths and compensates for their difficulties.

What you need to learn

- Decline in memory.
- Decline in reasoning and communication.
- Changes in behaviour.
- Loss of skills to carry out daily activities.

Decline in memory

Memory loss is a very common symptom and is often the first sign of dementia. Many people with dementia forget information that is required to carry out everyday tasks. However, the long-term memory of most individuals is still intact. This means that different activities, such as reminiscence, can still be used to stimulate and support individuals.

How memory loss affects people

Memory problems might affect an individual with dementia in the following ways. An individual might:

- put something away and forget where it is (sometimes they might think that someone has stolen it)
- forget how to find their way around
- be unable to follow a conversation
- be disorientated in time and place, e.g. think day is night
- forget significant events in their life
- have difficulty learning new things.

A memory test for a person with memory problems might be to ask them to recall three objects that they were shown only a few minutes previously.

An individual with dementia may:

- ask things repeatedly
- become anxious because they can't remember what to do next
- try to make something up because they can't remember (this is called confabulation).

Activity 28

We all have times in our lives when we forget things. Think about a time when one of the situations in the table below happened to you. Write down the feelings you had.

Situation	Your feelings
Met someone you knew in the street but couldn't remember their name.	
Lost your keys.	
Couldn't remember if you turned the oven/iron off or locked the front door.	

Now imagine having these feelings on an hourly or minute-by-minute basis.

Memory loss can be very upsetting and frustrating

Things that are not helpful

- Saying to a person with dementia, 'I just told you that'.
- Asking the person to stop repeating themselves.
- Refusing to clarify something every time it is requested.

Things that are helpful

- Technologies that prompt memory.
- Reminder sticky labels on things.
- Large clocks with easily readable numbers and dates.
- Reminder telephone calls.
- Offering reassurance where necessary.
- Providing information when asked.
- Repeating instructions.

Decline in reasoning and communication

One of the most obvious changes in a person with dementia is difficulties with communication. This has been covered in some detail on page 46. This may be demonstrated in very different ways and be complicated by other factors, such as poor sight or hearing. If someone has some difficulty with communication it can lead to a range of emotions, including anger and frustration. But there is much that you can do to support individuals who have communication difficulties.

Difficulties with understanding

This means that the person with dementia does not take in or understand the information the way that it is sent. Look back at page 47 to remind yourself of difficulties associated with understanding.

In order to help with difficulties in understanding you must make sure that you keep verbal language simple and, where needed, use non-verbal prompts.

> It is important to recognise that a person with dementia may be able to express themselves clearly but may have a lot of difficulty understanding you.

Difficulties with expression

This means that the person with dementia cannot represent their views clearly and it can be very frustrating for them. This might be shown in different ways (see page 47). You can help with this problem by developing your active listening skills. It is important also to take notice of the feelings behind the communication; the person's body language and tone.

Changes in behaviour

Changes in behaviour may occur as a consequence of the changes to the brain. Some types of dementia may be affected by this, for example Pick's disease in the changes occur to the frontal lobes of the brain which are responsible for our behaviour. Changes in behaviour may also be a response to inadequate and insensitive care or because of a person's inability to communicate their feelings. For example, an individual may become upset or angry because they are not understood or they have been ridiculed. Depression may lead to changes in behaviour as well; for example an individual may become socially withdrawn.

Types of behaviour change

Physical changes to the brain which cause behaviour changes may lead to the person with dementia:

- appearing selfish
- having mood swings
- becoming very uninhibited
- having aggressive outbursts
- performing obsessive compulsive activities
- repeating things over and over
- forming over-attachment bonds – following carers
- having hallucinations.

Such changes may be represented or viewed as negative changes. However some changes in behaviour may not be negative or challenging, and may be left to continue.

Challenging changes in behaviour can be very difficult for the person's carer to accept. However it is important to recognise that such changes are a consequence of the condition – the person did not choose to act in this way.

What you can do

There are some things that you can do to help with changes in a person's behaviour:

- understand what triggers the behaviour
- do not label people
- accept that your role is to care for someone not to change their behaviour
- do not challenge the person
- create a safe and understanding environment
- try to understand what the person is communicating.

Loss of skills to carry out daily activities

When a person with dementia loses the ability to carry out daily activities the experience can be profound. This was considered in the section on some of the losses that people with dementia experience (see page 18).

Daily activities might include:

- getting washed and dressed
- paying bills
- cooking a meal
- going on a journey.

There are different reasons why a person with dementia may be unable to carry out an activity, for example:

- difficulty in sequencing a task (for example, they are unable to determine the order of the activity, such as pouring the water out of the kettle before it has boiled)
- difficulty judging spaces (for example, they are unable to grasp objects effectively)
- lack of concentration (for example, they cannot stay focused on an activity for long enough)
- poor memory (they cannot remember the sequence of things)
- perceptual problems (for example, they cannot recognise objects).

All of the skills above are required to get up, get washed and get dressed. Not every person with dementia will be affected by every problem that is listed above. The key is to identify which area the person needs support with.

Activity 29

Think of someone who you are a carer for. In the table below, write in the left column their symptoms. Can you think of any symptoms that have not been covered so far? In the right-hand column, write what you do to support these symptoms.

Symptom	Activity to support
Example: Problems with coordination	*Example:* Prompt each stage of activity

4

Legislation and guidance relevant to individuals with dementia

4.1 Understand the legislation and guidance that is relevant to individuals with dementia

In this section you are going to learn about how legislation shapes areas of your work with people with dementia.

Legislation and people with dementia

It is important to have an understanding of how laws affect people with dementia because:

- you will come across issues in your work that relate to this guidance
- they underpin the policies and procedures that you have in your workplace
- you must ensure that the individual's rights are being upheld
- you must ensure that if rights are abused you know what the legal position is.

All legislation regarding the care of vulnerable people has basic values and principles which underpin it. For example, people with dementia have the right to:

- be protected from harm
- be treated with dignity and respect
- live as independent a life as possible
- be treated equally and be free from discrimination
- access the services that they need to support them.

All professionals working to support people with dementia should use the laws to guide them and provide them with a framework. However, it can be difficult to know your way around the legislation – particularly for people with dementia and their families. You, therefore, have a key role in offering advice and guidance to individuals and their families about their rights. You can provide information about where they can go to find out more about how the law can support them.

Individuals may need the protection of the law because:

- they need to make arrangements to manage their finances
- they need to make a decision but it is not clear that they have the mental capacity
- they have been kept in a residential home against their will
- they are being refused access to a service or funding for services
- they are being treated differently on the grounds of their dementia
- the care that they are receiving is not delivered to a specific standard
- the current situation is not safe.

1. Where can you advise a person with dementia or a family member to go to find out more about the law?

The Human Rights Act 1998

The origins of this act were set out in the Convention of Human Rights (European legislation). The Human Rights Act made this convention part of British law. The act sets out basic principles of fair treatment. If an individual feels that their rights have been breached by a public authority, or voluntary or private organisation, they can bring a case against them. This act has influence in all areas of health and social care and you will be affected by this in your work. Therefore as a carer you must work in accordance with the act. The act sets out the following principles:

- the right to life
- the right to freedom from torture and inhumane, degrading treatment
- the right to freedom from slavery and forced labour
- the right to liberty and security
- the right to have a fair trial
- no punishment without law
- the right to respect for private family life
- the right to freedom of thought, conscience and religion
- the right to freedom of expression
- the right to freedom of assembly and association
- the right to marry and have a family
- prohibition of discrimination.

In addition, the Human Rights Act incorporates new parts to the Convention:

- the protection of property
- the right to education
- the right to free elections
- the abolition of the death penalty.

The Mental Capacity Act 2005

The Mental Capacity Act is a new law that is being implemented in stages. The act was introduced to clarify some matters that were previously dealt with in the Mental Health Act 1983, including the assessment to determine someone's capacity. The act makes an important contribution to the protection of people with dementia as it starts from the premise that everyone has capacity to make decisions. Where it is deemed otherwise, the individual's wishes should still be represented by a skilled advocate. The main provisions of the Mental Capacity Act are as follows.

- The capacity test has to be based on the decision at issue – not on an overall capacity for decision making.
- Where it has been decided that someone does not have capacity regarding specific care and treatment, this can be delivered without the person becoming legally liable.
- Restraint can only be used where it is to prevent harm. The restraint used must be proportionate to the harm that is likely to occur.
- It allows the court to appoint someone to act on a person's behalf; this is called a Lasting Power of Attorney.
- It allows the court to appoint deputies who will make decisions about the person's welfare. This replaces the previous system called receivership in the Court of Protection.
- It creates two new public bodies – Court of Protection and Public Guardian.
- It appoints an Independent Mental Capacity Advocate to the person who lacks capacity and does not have anyone else to advocate for them.
- It allows people to make decisions in advance of their incapacity to refuse treatment and ensures that these decisions are subsequently upheld.
- It makes it a criminal offence for people to ill treat or neglect someone with dementia.
- Clear guidelines are provided for doing research on someone who lacks capacity.

You can find out more by visiting the website on the Mental Capacity Act. A link has been made available at www.heinemann.co.uk/hotlinks – just enter the express code 2307P.

The Enduring Power of Attorney Act 1985

The Enduring Power of Attorney Act gives a person with dementia a legal right to choose one or more people to act on their behalf to manage their financial affairs. The application for this can only be executed if the person still has the mental capacity to make decisions. Many people with a diagnosis of dementia have the mental capacity to make decisions, particularly in the early stages of the condition. Once an application has been made, the individual can continue to manage their own finances until they are no longer able to do so. A further notification is required at this stage.

These powers have been extended in the new Mental Capacity Act and the changes are due to be introduced in April 2007. These include a Lasting Power of Attorney which enables the person with dementia to empower someone to also have decision-making powers over their health and welfare. Currently this is only in place for decisions over finance and property.

The Community Care Act 1990

When this act was introduced it transformed the welfare state as it encouraged the use of private and voluntary services in delivering care in the community. Most significantly, the Community Care Act 1990 places a legal duty on the local authority to carry out assessments of need and to ensure that there is fair and equitable access to services. The local authority social services department is also responsible for producing a care plan that details how services will meet an individual's need. These services might include home care, day care, respite care, residential care, adaptations and equipment. The aim is to enable people to live as independently as possible within the community.

The Mental Health Act 1983

This act governs the assessment and treatment of people with mental health problems. It created powers to compulsorily admit a person with a mental health diagnosis to hospital for treatment and assessment. This power is typically used with other mental health conditions but can also be used with people who have a diagnosis of dementia. The act also sets out after care provisions. The act has several other powers, including the power to appoint a guardian. If a guardian is appointed, they can request the person to live at a certain address and request them to attend a specific place at a specific time, for example, to attend treatment. However, even though the act can request that person to attend a specific appointment it does not have the power to enforce treatment on an individual.

The Health Act 1999

This act introduced the pooling of budgets between the health and social care services. This is important as it has encouraged more joint working between health and social care, which is vital in the care of people with dementia. Before this, it was much less clear whether the care of people with dementia was the responsibility of the health authority or social services.

The National Service Framework for Older People

This framework sets out good practice guidance in the care of older people. National Service Frameworks have also been developed in other areas such as mental health, palliative care, cancer, diabetes, coronary heart disease and long-term conditions. The framework for older people sets out eight main areas for improvement:

1. rooting out age discrimination
2. person-centred care
3. intermediate care
4. general hospital care
5. stroke
6. falls
7. mental health in older people
8. the promotion of health and active life in older age.

The Care Standards Act 2000

The Care Standards Act was the biggest reform to care services since the introduction of the Community Care Act ten years earlier. The Care Standards Act created minimum standards of care for all care service providers. The minimum standards cover a wide range of issues in the delivery of care. The act also established the Commission of Social Care Inspectorate – the government body responsible for licensing and inspecting care. This act replaces licensing provisions under the Children's Act 1989, the Registered Homes Act 1984 and the Nursing Agency Act 1957.

The extract below shows Standard 18 regarding protection from abuse.

Commission of Social Care Inspectorate

Protection
OUTCOME: Service users are protected from abuse.
STANDARD 18

- *18.1 The manager makes sure that the service user is protected from abuse*

- *18.2 There are procedures in place that follow legislative guidance*

- *18.3 All abuse reports are followed up quickly and recorded*

- *18.4 Staff who are suspected of abuse are referred for inclusion on the protection of vulnerable adults register*

- *18.5 There is clear guidance on how to assess and manage aggressive incidents, and physical intervention is a last resort*

- *18.6 The home makes sure that when supporting someone with money they have clear procedures in place to reduce the risks*

The Data Protection Act 1998

The Data Protection Act covers how organisations collect, store, process and destroy information. The act enables people to have access to their own records and requires organisations to make this possible. The act aims to ensure the confidentiality of information and is the basis of policies for all types of organisations.

The Disability Discrimination Act 1995

This piece of legislation has been amended and developed over the last ten years to more accurately reflect the needs of society. This act makes it unlawful to discriminate against a person because of their disability and defines disability both in physical and mental terms. It breaks this down into categories and includes discrimination in employment as well as in the delivery of services.

Activity 30

In the table below write down how the different acts affect your work either directly or indirectly. Next think about how each act supports the person with dementia.

Legislation	How it affects your work	How it supports the person with dementia
Human Rights Act 1998		
Mental Capacity Act 2005		
Enduring Power of Attorney Act 1985		
Community Care Act 1990		
Mental Health Act 1983		
Health Act 1999		
National Service Framework for Older People		
Care Standards Act 2000		
Data Protection Act 1998		
Disability Discrimination Act 1995		

What you need to learn

- The role of policies and procedures.
- How policies are applied to working with people with dementia.

The role of policies and procedures

In your workplace you are required to work within the guidance of policies and procedures. These provide you with the aims of the organisation and detail what is required to achieve them. The detailed processes that are written down are called procedures. Policies and procedures are underpinned by legislation and the values of the organisation.

In your induction you will learn about your organisation's policies and procedures. This helps you to understand how your role fits into the organisation as a whole. It is important that you refer to them whenever you need clarification.

If you are not aware of your organisation's polices and procedures you might be at risk of:

- working in a different way to everyone else and therefore not working as a team
- not using safe systems at work and as a consequence putting yourself and the individual in your care at risk
- not being able to achieve organisational objectives
- presenting the organisation to others in an unprofessional way.

How policies are applied to working with people with dementia

The needs of people with dementia are complex and you may be faced with ethical dilemmas in your work. In these circumstances, as well as talking to the colleagues in your team, you should use your organisation's policies to guide you to make the correct decision. An organisation's policies and procedures will vary and therefore it is important to become familiar with these every time you start at a new place of work.

Activity 31

Each of the policies listed in the table below are important when working with people who have dementia. Write in the space next to the policy how you think it applies to a person with dementia.

Find out if there are any policies where you work that have not been included in the list in Activity 31.

Policy	How it applies to a person with dementia
Communicable diseases and infection control	
Confidentiality	
Procedure on the management of challenging behaviour	
Fire safety procedure	
Safe administration of medication	
Record keeping and access to files	
Health and safety	
Moving and handling	
Dealing with accidents and emergencies	
Responding to abuse	

Trainer notes

All care workers are required to develop knowledge-based skills and interpersonal skills. When undertaking training in dementia care, the emphasis initially has to be on the latter. As a facilitator, your primary role is to encourage your trainees to challenge their basic assumptions and beliefs. This process may be uncomfortable and difficult, and may require lengthy periods of reflection. These skills sets highlight the developing work into a strengths-based approach to dementia care. They present an exciting opportunity to be part of the evolution of dementia care and challenge us to consider the responsibility we have for the way our behaviour impacts on the people that we care for. Trainees should be given lots of opportunities to relate to their own experiences.

Before starting a session agree the boundaries of the session. This is defined within a learning contract. This enables the trainees and the trainer to work within agreed boundaries, and sets out the dos and don'ts of the session. The learning contract should encompass, as a very minimum, the importance of:

- confidentiality throughout the session
- timekeeping
- making connections with their own practice (reflective practice)
- agreeing to listen when other people are speaking and not to talk over other people
- challenging the statement and not the person. This is to encourage people to challenge in an appropriate de-personalised manner that enables constructive criticism.

This contract should be negotiated and owned by the trainees. Ask trainees to consider their past experiences in training, what worked well and what hindered the process. Encourage the trainees to use this experience to develop this learning contract.

1. Support individuals with dementia

1.1 Understand the need for a person-centred and strengths-based approach to the support and well-being of individuals with dementia

This section (pages 2–63) guides trainees through the ways in which they can support a person with dementia. You may wish to start a session with the following warm-up activity, which will encourage trainees to start working together and to explore some common assumptions. These assumptions might include:

- not consulting a person with dementia about their care because they are seen as incapable of making decisions
- being reluctant to engage because of differences in communication.

Ask trainees to turn to the person next to them and find out what that person has assumed about their life just by looking at them. This could be about lifestyle, family, hobbies, likes and dislikes. Trainees can then find out if their assumptions were correct. Explain that these assumptions will not be shared with the group.

Activity 1

As an alternative to the activity on page 3, put the statement written in the words of someone who has dementia on an OHP. Pull out each sentence and ask the trainees how these sentences make them feel. Try to prompt the following ideas:

- that our assumptions affect our behaviour
- that it is important to have empathy with people with dementia
- that it is important to understand the impact of dementia.

Activity 2

This activity could be performed as a group activity, and can be broadened by asking trainees to consider how their actions might impact on the rights of the individual, for example:

Word	Actions	Rights
Helpless	Do everything for the person	Loss of their independence and decision-making/choice

Summarise by explaining that a lot of harm can be done to someone who has dementia without realising it. The myths on page 4 can be used to explore common assumptions.

Activity 3

This activity gets trainees to question perceptions they might have about how a person with dementia should look. Encourage the connection between this exercise and the warm-up.

Activity 4

This activity considers the practical application of promoting rights. Common scenarios should be used to support this process, such as when delivering personal care to someone. This activity could be extended by asking trainees to consider what barriers exist in promoting rights. This can be looked at on a personal and organisational level, for example:

Personal barriers to promoting rights	Organisational barriers to promoting rights
Lack of understanding	Lack of resources to take a patient approach
Negative assumptions	Lack of training about communication needs
Not enough information about a person's abilities and strengths	Lack of clarity on the organisation's procedures when dealing with conflict and choices about taking risks

The Reflection on page 9 should be used to encourage trainees (working individually then feeding back to the group) to consider the consequences of overriding someone's rights. Case studies could be used to encourage debate which should reflect the diverse culture in society. However, real work experience will enable them to reflect. Trainees should be encouraged to respond that the person with dementia may become deskilled, withdrawn, angry and powerless. In turn, the carer may have no job satisfaction, may not be fulfilling their job role and may be overriding people's rights.

Role play may also be used to encourage this line of thinking. After the role play, ask the trainees to consider how they felt, from the perspective of both a carer and the individual with dementia. When facilitating a role play ensure that trainees are adequately briefed about the roles. Some trainees may find role play uncomfortable, but this is more likely where it is a new group and there are no established relationships. It is important to consider whether role play is appropriate within that group or at that stage of the group's life.

A presentation can be given on how trainees can support people to make choices about their care. You can do this by using the text on page 10. Encourage trainees to consider that by understanding people's needs and abilities better, they are enabled to support individuals in the decision-making process.

The Reflection on page 10 is designed to encourage trainees to consider the interplay between choices, communication and taking risks. In the feedback encourage the following points:

- where trainees can get support
- local procedures in documenting and reporting incidents

- the need to understand the underlying needs and wishes of people with dementia.

Activity 5

This activity encourages trainees to consider that choices can be made by behaviours and support may be needed to understand these behaviours better. Encourage trainees to use one of the scenarios that they are familiar with. In the feedback encourage trainees to recognise the importance of:

- responding calmly
- recognising underlying emotions that may drive an individual's choice
- reporting and recording concerns.

To extend this exercise, a role play could be used to enable trainees to practise their skills in responding to behaviours and to encourage empathy with people with dementia.

Care scenario: Amy

This scenario is designed to enable trainees to understand capacity, choices and the need for comprehensive risk assessments. Before completing the Care scenario, trainees will require some input on capacity and the processes used to determine it. The Mental Capacity Act can be used to explain the processes involved. Only the relevant areas of the act should be used in order not to overload the trainees.

1. Amy has the right to refuse her food where she understands the consequences of this.

2. Amy may be at risk of: malnutrition, social withdrawal, diminishing mobility, reduced skills in dressing and pressure

sores. Some of the physical risks may also lead to a confusional state.

3. Professionals who may help trainees to understand the risks better include: a psychologist (social withdrawal), a physiotherapist (diminishing mobility), an occupational therapist (reduced skills in dressing), a nurse (pressure sores) and a dietician (malnutrition).

Before completing the following Care scenario and Activity 6, trainees need to understand the basis of the social model of care (see page 14).

Care scenario: Mary

This Care scenario encourages trainees to consider how they can promote communication, empathy and trust in relationships with people with dementia.

1. Mary's behaviour suggests that she is distressed whilst being helped to dress.

2. The carer can help Mary not get so distressed by changing the way she helps Mary get dressed.

3. Mary is probably experiencing anger because she feels someone is overriding her rights.

Activity 6

Encourage the following points:

- recognising that we all hold assumptions is the first step to not allowing them to affect the way that we develop relationships

- the more we know about the person that we care for, the more common ground we can identify

- the more we understand about a person's abilities, the more likely we are to be able to engage with them in a mutually comfortable way.

Activity 7

Carrying out this activity in small groups enables trainees to broadly classify the losses experienced by people with dementia into psychological, physical and social categories. The relationships between the losses can also be explored, for example, a loss in memory functions (psychological) will impact on developing relationships (social). Using the illustration on page 18 on an OHP would be useful.

4. You can demonstrate that you understand what Mary is going through by telling her so, using appropriate communication techniques (e.g. reassuring language, holding her hand etc.).

5. You can gain Mary's trust by recognising and responding to her feelings, and doing things at her pace.

The Reflection on page 18 is designed to encourage the trainees to understand the personal experience of loss. This should be facilitated with sensitivity and caution. When feeding back from this exercise the trainer must highlight that:

- unlike our experiences, the individual with dementia is not able to draw on personal resources to comprehend the loss and manage the change

- understanding and support from the carer can help minimise the impact of this.

Care scenario: John

1. John has faced the loss of his home, his independence, his freedom to make choices, and also a loss of community/family relationships.

2. John experienced shock and denial.

The following Care scenario and Activity 8 should be completed when trainees have had the opportunity to understand what situations prompt assessment (page 22).

Care scenario: Rachel

1. Steps that trainees could take to build up a picture of Rachel's life could include speaking to family and friends. In addition, the photos themselves as well as the use of smells or music can help prompt memories.

2. Rachel's inclusion in the process of assessment could be supported by using different ways of portraying information, such as a picture storyboard.

Activity 8

This activity demonstrates the wide network of formal and informal carers who are involved in an individual's care and how this resource can be used to aid the assessment process.

The Reflection on page 25 encourages trainees to have a positive and progressive outlook on the care of people with dementia. It should encourage the candidates to take an empowering approach.

Activity 9

This activity encourages trainees to appreciate the importance of understanding strengths in order to build on these within a care plan. Trainees may have some difficulty completing this as they often consider strengths to be of a higher order and complexity. Encourage them to think about basic strengths that we may take for granted (examples can be found on page 25).

1.2 Understand the need to support and work with family and friends of the individual

The Reflection on page 26 asks trainees to relate to their own personal family experiences of dementia. This needs to be facilitated sensitively, reminding trainees of the learning contract. In the absence of this, the quote on page 26 can be used to encourage discussion about the experience of families. Feedback should include the importance of having an educative role with family members; this should be illustrated by the section on explaining person-centred care to families on page 26.

Care scenario: Maria

Trainees may need to carry out some research into what additional support services are available in order to complete this Care scenario. The scenario can also be adapted to more closely reflect local services.

1.3 Understand the need to protect the individual from abuse, injury and harm

The subject matter of abuse requires sensitivity and tact, and should be facilitated with care. It is important that you encourage trainees to think about the diverse society that we live in and you should not reinforce any negative stereotypes. Furthermore, dementia is a condition which may affect both young and old, and where possible case studies should be used to reflect this. This training should be complemented by mandatory Protection of Vulnerable Adults Training.

Activity 10

This activity will help trainees develop a knowledge of the signs of abuse. The activity can be completed in small groups with one trainee nominated to give the group's feedback. Trainees can find discussing sexual abuse within a group setting difficult and therefore it may be more appropriate to discuss only other types of abuse. Ensure that discussion covers the following points:

- people with dementia may experience multiple abuses
- the importance of understanding behaviours and therefore recognising where there have been changes
- the importance of following appropriate procedures in the recording and reporting of abuse.

To develop discussion further, ask candidates to consider the use of over-medication or to complete a role play where an individual is being detained against their will within a residential setting.

Activity 11

Trainees are encouraged to consider the causes of abuse and therefore to develop preventative strategies. This exercise covers a number of areas: the interpersonal, the organisational and the wider contexts of society. Sufficient time needs to be given to fully explore the issues which should be built on further in specific training sessions on the protection of vulnerable adults. Ensure that the following points are covered:

- the need to support informal carers on educative, emotional and practical levels
- how our assumptions influence behaviours and perceptions about power structures between the carer and the individual with dementia
- the importance of understanding aggression as a form of communication in order to prevent triggers of abuse
- the need to have personal responsibility to apply learning and awareness from training sessions to real contexts
- the importance of completing person-centred assessments and how this can prevent the individual's rights from being overridden, for example, their right to independence.

Care scenario: Paula

This Care scenario is designed to help trainees understand the benefits of advocacy where difficult decisions are required that may include an element of risk. Trainees can explore the difficulty posed when family members present the individual's rights, particularly where they have their own agenda and are emotionally involved – which can cause conflict.

1. The danger of asking Jane about Paula's wishes is that Jane may not give an accurate picture of Paula's wishes (Jane may not know, she may misunderstand or she may have her own wishes that are different to her mother's).

2. Jane may be overly concerned about any risks to her mother, whereas Paula may be able to see a balance between risks and the quality of her life.

3. Paula may be more honest with an independent advocate about the fact she does not want to leave her home.

4. An independent advocate will not be as emotionally involved as someone like Jane and so will be able to represent Paula's wishes for her.

Activity 12

The objective of this activity is to raise awareness of how assistive technologies can promote independence as well as reduce risks.

The Reflection on page 34 asks trainees to apply their knowledge to their own care environment. Encourage them to think individually about simple and effective changes such as keeping the area clutter-free and ensuring that there are no frequent changes to the environment.

Activity 13

Before completing this activity, present on an OHP common reasons why individuals may be at increased risk of falls. Ensure that you highlight that a person with dementia is twice as likely to fall as an older person without dementia. Completion of the table within Activity 13 (either individually or in groups) encourages trainees to think about the multi-play of factors that influence falls, i.e. the environment, the individual and other people. The completed table can be used to examine the factors before, during and after an incident and how this information would support the completion of a risk assessment. After the exercise, it is essential to highlight that failure to minimise the risk of falls could lead to an individual being admitted to hospital. Hospitals are very confusing places for a person with dementia and can cause further deterioration and admission to a residential home.

1.4 Understand the importance of maintaining the general good health and well-being of the individual with dementia

Activity 14

Trainees are encouraged to consider the many factors that influence meeting the nutritional needs of a person with dementia. If the trainee is not able to carry out this activity on an individual with whom they are working, a case study can be used. To develop the exercise further, you could ask the trainee where they would go to seek advice on questions that were out of their sphere of competence.

Care scenario: Rasheed

This Care scenario asks trainees to consider how having an unclean environment can lead to physical health problems. It also highlights the difficulty of raising concerns about personal care with a person with dementia.

1. Rasheed's dementia has caused physical changes in his brain. These changes have lead to a decrease in his motivation, which has lead to his poor personal hygiene and his current health problems.

2. The GP should be contacted so that Rasheed's chest infection can be treated as soon as possible. This should help with his confusion and agitation. It is important that Rasheed is diagnosed early so that proper support services and advice can be accessed. Rasheed and his wife will probably benefit from visits from carers, who can offer support with personal care and give advice relating to Rasheed's diagnosis.

Care scenario: Faridah

The Care scenario involving Faridah enables trainees to consider how mental, physical and social abilities impact on an individual's support needs with personal care. This framework can also be applied to other case studies. To extend this exercise you could add additional columns to see how rights, health and safety, and communication needs are influenced in each activity. A further column could include the perspective of the person with dementia. Two examples are given below.

1.5 Understand the need for a positive and effective communication with the individual with dementia

The Reflection on page 47 asks trainees to make links with their own experiences to see if there is any correlation between the common communication problems listed and the difficulties experienced by the individual they work with. This Reflection also asks trainees to think about what strategies they have adopted to overcome some of these difficulties. The key message from this activity is to ask trainees if they took account of the feelings behind the expression when trying to understand what the individual was communicating. Highlight to trainees that feelings are real and should be listened to.

Need	How this will be supported	Health and safety	Communication	Individual's perspective
Faridah has some memory problems	Faridah will be prompted in stages to carry out her personal care independently	Ensure that Faridah is reminded to take additional care during risky activities, such as transfers on slippery floors	Use short and simple sentences when prompting	Faridah believes that she has already had a wash
Faridah has some problematic areas of skin	Cream to be applied to this area	This needs to be regularly monitored particularly when Faridah refuses to have a bath	When applying cream explain to Faridah what it is for	Faridah believes that she can care for her skin herself

Care scenario: Jean

This Care scenario highlights different perspectives and how these can influence behaviour. Use the Care scenario to encourage trainees to develop their empathy skills and try to see the situation from the individual's perspective. This is a common scenario and therefore trainees might want to use real experiences on which to base their learning.

1. Jean was probably not feeling in control of what was happening to her.

2. Jean may be thinking that a stranger has come into her room and assaulted her.

3. The carer should have made more effort to talk to Jean and not just started undressing her. The carer should have stopped when Jean started shouting and talked to Jean again.

Activity 15

As an alternative, role play can be used to complete this activity. Make sure that you rotate the trainees so that they both experience the bad listening. There needs to be plenty of time for reflection. After the activity make sure that you cover the following points:

- reflection on the experience of not being listened to. Ask trainees to think about the consequences of this on a long-term basis

- the pressures of work may lead carers to behave in this way without consciously recognising this, e.g. during busy times such as mornings or lunchtimes

- good listening techniques (see page 51).

The Reflection on page 49 asks trainees to reflect on a challenging incident. To develop discussion further you could ask trainees to consider what happened before, during and after the incident. Trainees should consider what factors influenced the behaviour. These could be environmental difficulties or differences in perspectives which are combined with poor communication techniques.

Activity 16

This activity is designed to help trainees experience the use of personal space during communications. A practical demonstration should be carried out in class by the trainer. Divide the group into pairs again to carry out this exercise. In the feedback ensure that you cover:

- the need for body spacing to create a sense of partnership working, and respect

- how by standing over someone the care worker creates a sense of power and disrespect

- that cultural needs will influence personal space.

Activity 17

This activity can be used to highlight the importance of tone when communicating. If a person with dementia is unable to pick up the content of the communication, they are often able to pick up the tone. To extend this activity, ask the trainees to note the body language that is used when presenting these different feelings.

Activity 18

This activity is designed to enable trainees to think about the uniqueness of each individual's communication needs. The activity uses case studies that highlight how both physical and mental health needs impact on communication. The types of communication listed enable trainees to think critically about the appropriateness of each method given the variety of communication needs.

After this activity, ensure that you:

- cover that there are a number of factors which influence communication that are common with people with dementia, such as sensory deficits due to old age and vascular problems. It is important to remind the group that not all people with dementia are elderly and therefore no assumptions should be made about communication needs, and so every case should be treated differently

- present the techniques on page 55. Allow plenty of time for this.

1.6 Understand that activities, therapies and medication may be used to help individuals with dementia

Activity 19

The assessment guide given in this exercise is designed specifically to identify how appropriate an activity is for a person with dementia. This tool can be used with an individual who the trainees are currently working with or a case study. If the trainees are not able to answer some of the questions, suggest to them where they might be able to get the information from. Once the activity is completed compare the assessment to a range of activities to see if it fits

In the feedback from the session ensure that you cover:

- the need to assess each individual, rather than putting them together in a group activity

- the consequences of having someone take part in an activity that they are unable to engage with

- the importance of historical information in an assessment

- the importance of building on strengths during an activity .

Activity 20

This activity is designed to encourage trainees to consider what techniques might be used to deliver sensory therapy. Trainees may be limited by the resources available to them but it is important to encourage them to think creatively. You should encourage the trainee to think about the different types of complementary therapies available and issues to consider in the delivery of each of the therapies.

Activity 21

As an alternative to this activity, you can provide a group of trainees with one role from those listed on pages 64–7 (may be on a laminated card). Ask the group to stand in a circle and show each of their colleagues what their role is. Explain that the object of the game is to get everyone sitting down. Tell them that they will need to discuss between themselves which is the correct role for the need listed in the table. This group activity encourages team work and should be used to build the development of the group.

2. Roles, responsibilities and boundaries

2.1 Understand the roles, responsibilities and boundaries of individuals and how team work and support can lead to better support of individuals with dementia

In this section (pages 64–77) trainees will learn about the many people, services and organisations who work as a team providing care to someone with dementia. This includes an understanding of their own role, responsibilities and boundaries as a care worker.

2.2 Understand the importance of communicating, reporting and recording effectively in the care environment

Before starting Activities 22 and 23, make sure that you cover the reasons why we record (see page 68). These can be put on an OHP or you could get ideas from the trainees.

Activity 22

This activity enables trainees to consider the consequences of not making recordings and can be completed individually or in groups. When giving feedback at the end of the activity, make sure that you cover:

- risks
- learning about and understanding the individual's needs
- accountability
- consistency.

Activity 23

The purpose of this activity is to enable trainees to understand the difference between fact and opinion in recordings.

Activity 24

This activity enables trainees to think about the different purposes of records and the consequences that can occur if they are not read. In the feedback ensure that you cover the importance of:

- understanding the purpose of a record before carrying out any recordings
- avoiding duplication
- issues of confidentiality.

Activity 25

This activity illustrates how a different perspective can influence recordings, which in turn will influence the reader's view. Trainees could work in small groups for this activity and will need plenty of time for reflection afterwards. In the feedback ensure that you cover:

- fact and opinion
- the consequences to the reader
- language used
- the importance of recording strengths.

2.3 Understand the roles and responsibilities of services and organisations in relation to dementia care

Ensure that the following are covered:

- the continuum of services
- the experience for the individual of different settings
- the importance of preventing admission to residential settings by taking an empowering approach.

3. Defining dementia

3.1 Understand the definition of dementia and the difference between dementia, depression and confusional states. Understand the importance of diagnosis and the implications for support and the care of the individual

This section (pages 78–89) details the different causes of dementia and explains some of the differences and similarities between them. The trainee will also look at other conditions that can be similar to dementia and, by the end of the section, should understand why correct diagnosis is so important.

Before starting Activity 26, ensure that trainees have read and understood the definitions given on pages 83–5. The activity will not be effective if trainees do not grasp the differences in these conditions.

Activity 26

After the activity, ensure that you discuss:

- how every individual is unique, therefore, when planning care, information about the diagnosis should be delivered in context with the person's wishes, life history and personality

- that there are places where trainees can go to get specific advice about the different dementias.

3.2. Understand the most common types and causes of dementia

This section is designed to introduce trainees to some of the most common forms of dementia. Statistical data can be presented usefully at this stage, for example, it is important that trainees are made aware that 55 per cent of the dementia population have Alzheimer's, as opposed to 20 per cent who have a vascular dementia. The illustration on page 82 shows how dementia is the umbrella term for different types of dementia. Ensure trainees have seen this, as many people get confused about the terms used. Understanding the physiological changes in the brain can be complex and is not necessary at this level. More focus should be given to the symptoms and the implications that these have for care.

This section should *not* be delivered as the first session. This is because it is important that the trainee understands the person before the diagnosis.

The Reflection on page 83 asks trainees what might happen if they were diagnosed with a form of dementia. As a variation of this, you could ask trainees to consider

what they would want to find out if a member of their family were diagnosed.

Before starting Activity 27, ensure that trainees have read and understood the definitions given on pages 83–5 and briefly explain the process of diagnosis. It is important to focus on:

- the role of trainees in providing information to allied medical staff on the symptoms that are presented

- the role of families in providing an historical perspective of the symptoms

- the experience of diagnosis for the individual.

Activity 27

This activity is designed to help trainees think about the differences in types of dementia and what the implications are for care. After the activity ensure that you cover the following points:

- younger people will have different needs in their lives that must be met

- the speed of the deterioration will have an impact on the frequency of the reviews

- the nature of the deterioration will impact on how care is planned, for example, if a person with a step-wise deterioration has an incident which triggers this, the care plan may need to be altered at the same time to reflect the change in abilities

- identifying what strengths remain can help to maximise abilities, for example, in some of the frontal lobe dementias, orientation and memory may be more intact

- the progression of the symptoms for a particular condition will help the individual and family to plan the care better.

3.3 Understand the common signs and symptoms of dementia

Activity 28

This activity is designed to encourage trainees to empathise with individuals with dementia by identifying common feelings. Other common scenarios can be used. While this activity can be completed in small groups it is important that each person in the group has experienced the scenario in order for them to reflect on their own feelings. After this activity ensure that you encourage candidates to consider how certain emotions may lead to challenging behaviours, particularly where there are communication difficulties.

Activity 29

This activity is designed to encourage trainees to develop strategies for supporting some of the symptoms of dementia. The activity can be performed with a group of trainees, ensuring that discussion is encouraged. Make sure that throughout this exercise there is a clear focus on what symptoms are as a result of a dementia, as opposed to other factors. Where such instances arise, they should be used as discussion points. This exercise is a good opportunity for trainees to learn practical tips on how to support individuals.

Ensure that throughout the activity trainees have considered supporting individuals with dementia in a way that:

- values their individuality
- maximises their independence
- makes the most of their strengths
- is not degrading or disrespectful in any way.

4. Legislation and guidance relevant to individuals with dementia

4.1 Understand the legislation and guidance that is relevant to individuals with dementia

In this section (pages 90–7) trainees will learn about some significant pieces of legislation and how they apply when working with people who have dementia.

Before starting Activity 30, you should ensure trainees have read the information regarding the different pieces of legislation (pages 91–5). Alternatively, you could present this information to them using an OHP. Trainees are not required to have an in-depth knowledge of the laws, but must understand what the legislation is trying to achieve.

Activity 30

Trainees are asked to think about how legislation applies to their day-to-day work, either directly or indirectly, and how it supports the individuals in their care. It may also be useful to discuss how certain items of legislation may be more applicable within certain roles, for example, where a care worker is working in the community as opposed to working in a residential setting.

4.2 Understand the organisation's policies and procedures and how to apply them with regard to people with dementia

Activity 31

This activity is designed to enable trainees to demonstrate their knowledge of policies within their workplace and to discuss how these apply to working with people with dementia. This activity can be extended to discuss wider practice issues that relate to the care of people with dementia. In the wider discussion ensure that you cover the importance of working with policies and the consequences of not working within the scope of this guidance.

Student log

The following tables have been reproduced with the kind permission of Skills for Care. Use these tables to log your progress during your training and record the learning outcomes you have covered. The tables may also be used to map the content of an NVQ qualification or other relevant training course. For full details of how the knowledge set for dementia cross-references NVQ units, Common Induction Standards and GSCC Code of Practice (workers), please see the Skills for Care knowledge set document. A link to the documents on the skillsforcare.org.uk website has been made available at www.heinemann.co.uk/hotlinks. Simply enter the express code 2307P when you access the site.

Main area	Learning outcome	Learning outcome achieved (manager's or trainer's signature)	Date
1. Support of individuals with dementia	1.1 Understand the need for a person-centred and strengths-based approach to the support and well-being of individuals with dementia: ▪ Value and accept the individual by seeing the person first and the dementia second ▪ Communicate effectively so that the individual has the opportunity to make decisions ▪ Where an individual cannot make a decision about their own care or welfare, the worker should act in their best interests and in the least restrictive manner ▪ Develop a person-to-person relationship with the individual ▪ Involve the individual with dementia in their own care planning ▪ Take account of history (personal, family, medical, etc.) and work towards meeting the needs of the whole person ▪ Adhere to the value base of care (identity, dignity, respect, choice, independence, privacy, rights, culture)		

Main area	Learning outcome	Learning outcome achieved (manager's or trainer's signature)	Date
	■ Take account of the individual's personal beliefs including spiritual beliefs, emotional needs and preferences ■ Maintain a responsive and flexible approach to the individual, taking account of changing needs ■ Take account of some of the feelings and issues that are commonly experienced by people with dementia, for example, around loss (of control, community, etc.)		
	1.2 Understand the need to support and work with family and friends of the individual: ■ Develop their understanding of a person-centred approach to support and care of individuals with dementia ■ Provide information about services and support networks available (e.g. support groups, specialist organisations like Alzheimer's Society, etc.)		
	1.3 Understand the need to protect the individual from abuse*, injury and harm: ■ Staff awareness and training ■ Involving family and friends ■ Independent advocacy ■ Assistive technologies (pressure mats, door alarms linked to staff pagers, personal pendant alarms, colour-coded handrails, pictures/ images on doors)		

Main area	Learning outcome	Learning outcome achieved (manager's or trainer's signature)	Date
	▪ The effect an environment can have that includes space choice and access to gardens. An enabling and safe environment (circular paths, floor coverings/soft furnishings that are not heavily patterned, distinct difference between walls and ceilings through use of colours and textures, etc.) ▪ Awareness of the possibility of an increased risk of falls * Types of abuse include: physical, sexual, racist, emotional, financial, institutional, neglect.		
	1.4 Understand the importance of maintaining the general good health and well-being of the individual with dementia: ▪ Food, nutrition, eating and drinking at regular intervals ▪ Appropriate exercise and activities specific to the needs of the individual ▪ Personal care (including measures to reduce risk of infection*) ▪ Living in a clean and enabling environment * There may be a link between physical illness and confusion in some individuals. Some medication may add to confusion and/or agitation.		

Main area	Learning outcome	Learning outcome achieved (manager's or trainer's signature)	Date
	1.5 Understand the need for a positive and effective communication with the individual with dementia: ■ Recognise that the individual's behaviour will often be directly related to their need to communicate about their feelings and needs ■ Look and listen carefully and take account of what an individual is communicating ■ Respond appropriately and positively to an individual's various forms of communication (using non-threatening body language and tone of voice, use of simple sentences, being calm and unrushed) ■ Give encouragement and focus on the individual's strengths and abilities		
	1.6 Understand that activities, therapies and medication may be used to help individuals with dementia: ■ Conventional medicines ■ Complementary therapies and activities (herbal medicine, acupuncture, aromatherapy and massage, sensory therapy, music therapy, etc.)		

Main area	Learning outcome	Learning outcome achieved (manager's or trainer's signature)	Date
2. Roles, responsibilities and boundaries	2.1 Understand the roles, responsibilities and boundaries of individuals and how team work and support can lead to better support of individuals with dementia: ■ Individual ■ Family and friends of individual ■ Independent advocate ■ Care worker ■ Manager ■ Social worker ■ General Practitioner ■ Specialist personnel (psychiatrist, therapists, community psychiatric nurse)		
	2.2 Understand the importance of communicating, reporting and recording effectively in the care environment: ■ Distinguish between subjective and objective language, fact and opinion ■ Use clear, objective statements in care plans, reports, daily logs, handover reports, etc. ■ The use of appropriate language and to avoid the use of negative statements and language when describing a person with dementia		

Main area	Learning outcome	Learning outcome achieved (manager's or trainer's signature)	Date
	2.3 Understand the roles and responsibilities of services and organisations in relation to dementia care: ■ Care homes with personal care or nursing care ■ Hospitals ■ Domiciliary, respite and day services ■ Sheltered accommodation and supported housing ■ Voluntary and charitable organisations (e.g. Alzheimer's Society, Mental Health Foundation, Age Concern, Anchor Trust, MIND)		
3. Defining dementia	3.1 Understand the definition of dementia and the difference between dementia, depression and confusional states. Understand the importance of diagnosis and the implications for support and care of the individual.		
	3.2 Understand the most common types and causes of dementia, for example: ■ Alzheimer's Disease ■ Vascular dementia ■ Pick's Disease (Fronto-Temporal) ■ Dementia with Lewy bodies ■ Creutzfeld Jakob Disease (CJD) ■ Huntington's Disease		

Main area	Learning outcome	Learning outcome achieved (manager's or trainer's signature)	Date
	3.3 Understand the common signs and symptoms of dementia, for example: ■ Decline in memory ■ Decline in reasoning and communication ■ Changes in behaviour ■ Loss of skills to carry out normal daily activities		
4. Legislation and guidance relevant to individuals with dementia	4.1 Understand the legislation and guidance relevant to individuals with dementia: ■ Human Rights Act 1998 ■ Mental Capacity Act 2005 ■ Enduring Power of Attorney Act 1985 ■ Community Care Act 1990 ■ Mental Health Act 1983 ■ Care Standards Act 2000 ■ Data Protection Act 1998 ■ Disability Discrimination Act 1995 ■ Health Act 1999 ■ National Service Framework for Older People N.B. This list of legislation and guidance is given as examples. Legislation and guidance is subject to change. It is important when designing learning packages, in-house training, etc., that the most recent legislation and guidance is included.		
	4.2 Understand the organisation's policies and procedures and how to apply them with regard to people with dementia, for example, visitor policy, no secrets policy		

Glossary

Abuse   intentional acts or omissions of care which lead to harm of a vulnerable person

Advocate   an independent person who works alongside an individual with dementia in order to help them get their view/opinion/decision across to others. Advocates do not make decisions for people

Alzheimer's disease   the most common form of dementia; a progressive condition where brain cells die

Capacity   the ability to make informed decisions

Confabulation   creating imaginary experiences to make up for loss of memory

Confusional state   a temporary condition caused by some sort of infection

Continuum of care/services   the range of services that is available to meet people's different needs

Disempowerment   the feeling that you have no power or control over what happens to you

Empowerment   having the opportunity and support to have choices and make decisions

Enable   to make something able to happen

Gait   the way a person walks

Holistic   an approach to care that treats the whole person, rather than just parts of them. Treating the whole person means taking into account their physical and mental health, their environment, their social network, emotional and spiritual factors etc.

Malnutrition   insufficient nutrition; where there is not the right food necessary for health

Multi-disciplinary team   a group of professionals from different disciplines (e.g. medicine, nursing, social work, occupational therapy) that are involved in the care of the same individual

Personal care   personal hygiene activities e.g. washing, bathing

Person-centred   care and support that is suited to an individual and their particular needs

Proactive   to plan ahead and take action before an event happens, as opposed to responding to the event

Rehabilitation   to restore a function (e.g. walking, talking) to a previous state

Value base of care   core values you need to adhere to, such as: non-judgemental, non-discriminatory, upholding people's rights

Index